CrewAI Framewc

Design and Deploy Advanced Multi-Agent AI Systems to Automate Complex Processes and Transform Workflows

Gilberto Neal

Copyright Page

Table of Contents

Introduction

Artificial intelligence has seen a rapid evolution over the past few years, driven in large part by large language models (LLMs) such as GPT, Claude, and others. These models have enabled powerful new capabilities in natural language understanding, generation, and task execution. However, while these models are effective at performing isolated tasks—such as summarizing text, generating code, or answering questions—they are not inherently structured for handling complex, multi-step processes that require coordination, memory, or role specialization.

This limitation has given rise to a new paradigm in AI system design: **multi-agent systems**. A multi-agent system is a framework where multiple autonomous agents interact, collaborate, or coordinate to achieve a set of goals. Each agent in the system is assigned a distinct role or responsibility, often tied to a particular function, such as research, planning, execution, or verification. Rather than relying on a single prompt to guide a monolithic model, multi-agent systems structure intelligent behavior through communication, delegation, and task distribution among agents.

The use of multiple agents introduces a modular architecture that mirrors how real-world teams operate. Just as human teams consist of specialists working together to solve complex problems, AI agents can be designed to specialize in certain types of thinking or behavior, and then communicate with other agents to solve problems that exceed the scope of any one model or function. This shift represents a significant advancement: it allows developers to build systems that are more adaptive, context-aware, and capable of handling real-world workflows that require coordination, not just computation.

What Is CrewAI?

CrewAI is a Python-based open-source framework specifically designed for building and coordinating multi-agent AI systems using LLMs. It provides a structured way to define agents, assign them tasks, equip them with tools, and coordinate their actions through customizable process handlers. CrewAI abstracts away much of the complexity involved in designing agent systems by providing clear primitives and workflows that make it easier to reason about task delegation and execution.

At its core, CrewAI introduces five main concepts: the **Agent**, **Task**, **Tool**, **Crew**, and **Process Handler**. An Agent is an autonomous unit with a defined role and capability. A Task is a specific objective assigned to an agent. A Tool is a functional component that an agent can use to perform actions—such as calling an API or querying a database. A Crew is a group of agents that work together to complete tasks. The Process Handler defines how the agents operate together—sequentially, in parallel, hierarchically, or using custom logic.

This book is written to provide developers with a complete, practical guide to understanding and applying the CrewAI framework. While introductory examples exist online, few resources explain how to design, optimize, and deploy robust agent-based systems for production use. This book fills that gap by focusing on real-world workflows, thoughtful design patterns, and techniques that will help you move from experimentation to implementation.

Who This Book Is For

This book is designed for software developers, AI engineers, and technical architects who want to build intelligent, autonomous systems using modern AI techniques. If you're comfortable with Python and have some familiarity with APIs or LLMs, you'll be able to follow the material and build advanced agent-based applications with confidence.

You don't need prior experience in agent modeling, robotics, or reinforcement learning to benefit from this book. CrewAI is designed to be accessible to developers who are new to multi-agent thinking, while still offering the flexibility and depth needed for advanced users who want to customize workflows or scale their agent systems.

Whether you're building task automation tools, intelligent assistants, internal AI platforms, or production-grade agent infrastructure, the content in this book will help you go beyond simple prompt engineering and move toward modular, agent-based system design.

How to Use This Book

This book is organized progressively to support both learning and reference. Early chapters focus on foundational concepts such as defining agents, creating tasks, and configuring tools. These chapters are written to give you hands-on experience quickly, with working examples that demonstrate core features of CrewAI.

As the book progresses, later chapters introduce more advanced topics such as coordination strategies, performance optimization, error handling, observability, and deployment. Throughout the book, real-world use cases and projects illustrate how CrewAI can be applied to solve problems in business intelligence, DevOps automation, content pipelines, and more.

You can read the book cover to cover to build up your understanding step-by-step, or you can skip directly to topics that are most relevant to your current needs. Every chapter is self-contained enough to be used as a guide when building or debugging specific parts of a CrewAI system.

All code samples are written in Python and designed to be easily adapted into your own projects. Where relevant, you'll find best practices, architectural advice, and commentary on trade-offs that will help you make better design decisions.

By the end of this book, you will be equipped to design, optimize, and deploy intelligent multi-agent systems using CrewAI with confidence and clarity.

Chapter 1: The Agent Paradigm Shift

AI is evolving—and quickly. What started with simple, single-step prompts to large language models (LLMs) has grown into something far more powerful and structured: systems of autonomous agents that can reason, act, collaborate, and accomplish real work. This chapter is your introduction to that shift.

We're going to take a close look at how and why developers are moving beyond one-off prompts and starting to build systems composed of intelligent agents. You'll learn what multi-agent systems are, how they work with LLMs, and what makes them fundamentally different from traditional prompt engineering. We'll also explore the broader landscape of agent coordination frameworks and clarify why CrewAI has quickly become one of the most accessible and flexible tools for developers building in this space.

From Prompts to Autonomous Agents

If you've worked with large language models like GPT-4 or Claude, you're already familiar with the standard workflow: you send a prompt, the model responds with a prediction. That interaction is simple and effective, especially when you're asking a model to write an email, generate a product description, or explain a piece of code. But as soon as your task grows in complexity—especially when it includes multiple steps, intermediate decisions, external data sources, or dependencies on previous actions—this prompt-and-response model starts to feel inadequate.

A prompt is just a single request to a model. The model sees that prompt, generates a response based on statistical patterns in its training data, and then forgets the whole exchange as soon as it's done. There's no memory, no self-direction, and no persistence beyond that one interaction. If you want the model to "remember" anything, you have to keep feeding it everything it might need on every request. That works for small tasks, but not when you're coordinating multi-step workflows or replicating decision-making over time.

Let's take a real example. Suppose you're building a tool that helps generate weekly SEO blog posts based on trending topics. The workflow might include these steps:

Query a search engine or news feed for trending keywords

Select one based on topic relevance

Research supporting facts or articles

Generate a draft blog post

Optimize it for keywords and readability

Format it for publishing

Now, doing all of that with a single prompt would be unrealistic. You'd need to call the model multiple times, each time providing context from the previous step, and manually orchestrating the process in your Python code. You might get by with some clever prompt chaining, but the moment you want the process to become flexible—maybe to retry failed steps, handle exceptions, or allow agent-to-agent collaboration—it becomes difficult to maintain.

This is exactly where the concept of an **autonomous agent** becomes useful.

An autonomous agent, in this context, is not just a wrapper around an LLM. It's a self-contained software entity with a defined role, a goal, access to tools, and the ability to make decisions based on context. Rather than being given a one-time prompt, it's assigned a task. It can think through that task, use the tools at its disposal, remember relevant information, and either execute the task or hand off parts of it to other agents. That's a much more powerful and scalable way to build AI systems.

Let's look at this in practice. Suppose we want to create a **ResearchAgent** whose job is to find and summarize trending AI news. Here's how that might look in CrewAI:

```python
from crewai import Agent, Task, Tool, Crew
from langchain.tools import DuckDuckGoSearchRun

search_tool = DuckDuckGoSearchRun()

research_agent = Agent(
    role='AI Researcher',
```

```
    goal='Summarize the most relevant news in the
AI industry this week',
    backstory='You are an expert AI researcher
known for identifying significant breakthroughs.',
    tools=[search_tool],
    verbose=True
)

research_task = Task(
    description='Search the web for current trends
in AI and summarize the three most important
developments.',
    expected_output='A short summary with bullet
points explaining each development.',
    agent=research_agent
)

crew = Crew(
    agents=[research_agent],
    tasks=[research_task],
    verbose=True
)

result = crew.run()
print(result)
```

In this example, we're not just sending a prompt to a model. We're defining an agent with a role, a goal, and a tool. The agent knows how to search the web, it understands what it's trying to accomplish, and it's assigned a task that matches its role. When `crew.run()` is called, the agent executes that task independently, using its tool and contextual understanding.

Notice how the process is now framed in terms of **roles and tasks**, not just inputs and outputs. This unlocks a lot of power. You could easily add a second agent—a **WriterAgent**—to take the output of the researcher and turn it into a blog post. Or a **FactCheckerAgent** to validate the claims. Each agent can specialize, work independently, and pass results to the next agent in the flow. That's coordination, not chaining.

Now let's add a **WriterAgent** and assign it a writing task. Here's how that might look:

```
writer_agent = Agent(
    role='Technical Content Writer',
    goal='Turn research into a clear, engaging blog
post for a general tech audience',
    backstory='You are a professional writer with
experience in simplifying complex AI topics.',
    verbose=True
)

writing_task = Task(
    description='Using the research summary, write
a 600-word blog post that introduces the three AI
developments in an engaging way.',
    expected_output='A ready-to-publish markdown-
formatted blog post.',
    agent=writer_agent,
    context=[research_task]  # Feed the output of
the first task as input
)

crew = Crew(
    agents=[research_agent, writer_agent],
    tasks=[research_task, writing_task],
    verbose=True
)

result = crew.run()
print(result)
```

Here, we're coordinating between two agents: the researcher does the information gathering, and the writer transforms it into an article. This mimics how real teams work. Each agent has a defined role, a task that matches its expertise, and access to relevant input from the other agents in the system. You don't need to manually prompt each one in sequence or figure out where to store intermediate results—it's all built into the agent-task-crew structure.

This way of working has some immediate benefits:

Modularity: You can reuse and swap agents or tasks without rewriting your whole process.

Clarity: Each part of the workflow is self-documenting. You can see exactly who does what and how.

Scalability: You can add more agents or parallelize tasks as needed.

Maintainability: Your system logic is easier to test, debug, and reason about.

To bring this closer to the real world, think about companies using AI to power editorial workflows, customer service operations, or technical documentation. Instead of relying on one giant prompt stuffed with context and tools, they're starting to think in terms of distributed systems—small, specialized agents doing focused tasks, all coordinated with lightweight, composable logic.

You're no longer just crafting clever prompts—you're designing intelligent systems.

The shift from prompting to agents is about introducing **structure, autonomy, and collaboration** into your AI systems. With agents, you're not just solving problems—you're building **problem solvers**. And that's a huge step forward in how we think about automation, productivity, and scalable AI development.

Understanding LLMs in Multi-Agent Contexts

To work effectively with multi-agent systems, you first need a solid understanding of how large language models (LLMs) behave when embedded within agent workflows. When used inside an agent, an LLM is not just responding to isolated prompts—it becomes part of a structured decision-making process, often in collaboration with other agents, tools, or external data sources.

Let's start with the fundamentals. An LLM such as GPT-4, Claude, or Mistral is essentially a very powerful text predictor. When you give it a prompt, it analyzes the text you've provided and generates a response by predicting the most likely next token based on patterns learned during training. This mechanism, while simple in theory, is capable of producing remarkably sophisticated outputs—from writing full essays to generating working code or simulating conversation.

But it's important to understand what the model **doesn't** do. It doesn't retain memory across interactions unless you design for it. It doesn't have goals. It doesn't know when it's made a mistake unless you tell it. It's not actively pursuing objectives—it's just completing sequences of text. When you use it inside an agent, your job is to give it structure, constraints, and context.

Now, when you bring LLMs into a **multi-agent system**, you're doing something very different from traditional prompting. You're not treating the model as a standalone assistant anymore. You're embedding it inside an agent, and then giving that agent a specific role, a goal, access to external tools, and often a set of instructions on how to interact with other agents or the outside world.

Let's look at a hands-on example that will help this come alive. Say you're building a system that performs market research and creates a competitor summary report. You want one agent to gather the data and another agent to write the report. You're using OpenAI's GPT-4 model to power both agents. Here's how this might be structured with CrewAI:

```
from crewai import Agent, Task, Crew
from langchain.tools import DuckDuckGoSearchRun

search_tool = DuckDuckGoSearchRun()

data_collector = Agent(
    role='Market Analyst',
    goal='Gather data about current competitors in
the AI space',
    backstory='You are skilled at finding relevant
and up-to-date market intelligence using search
engines and online data.',
    tools=[search_tool],
    verbose=True
)

report_writer = Agent(
    role='Business Writer',
    goal='Generate a clear summary of competitive
positioning in the AI market',
```

```
    backstory='You are a professional business
writer with a strong understanding of market
dynamics.',
    verbose=True
)

data_task = Task(
    description='Use the search tool to identify
and summarize at least three major AI companies,
focusing on their product offerings, recent moves,
and market strengths.',
    expected_output='A structured list of three
competitors, each with a summary of their latest
activities and positioning.',
    agent=data_collector
)

report_task = Task(
    description='Using the market summary, write a
concise business report that compares the strengths
and weaknesses of these competitors.',
    expected_output='A markdown-formatted report
with headings, competitor profiles, and a
concluding analysis.',
    agent=report_writer,
    context=[data_task]
)

crew = Crew(
    agents=[data_collector, report_writer],
    tasks=[data_task, report_task],
    verbose=True
)

result = crew.run()
print(result)
```

This example demonstrates how an LLM-powered agent behaves differently than a traditional prompt. Each agent is responsible for interpreting its task, understanding its role, and using the tools available to it. The LLM is not generating answers randomly—it is **interpreting its goal in the context of a structured task** and producing output accordingly. And because we feed the

15

output of one task into the next, the second agent can build on the context provided by the first.

This model also highlights a subtle but important shift in how you interact with LLMs. When used inside agents, prompts aren't static instructions—you're dynamically generating prompt templates based on the task's goal, the agent's role, and its available tools. CrewAI does this for you under the hood. That's one reason the `Agent`, `Task`, and `Crew` structures are so useful—they encapsulate the prompt logic and enforce a consistent pattern that reduces error and ambiguity.

In multi-agent systems, LLMs gain new capabilities because the environment around them provides the missing pieces: memory, coordination, feedback, and tool access. And because you can connect multiple agents together, each with its own LLM and tools, the entire system becomes much more than the sum of its parts.

For example, in a single-agent setup, the LLM might only have access to web search. But in a multi-agent setup, one agent could search, another could process financial data using a spreadsheet tool, and a third could write a summary—all independently powered by their own prompts, goals, and tools. And none of them needs to know how the others work—they just consume the output of the previous task, the same way people do in a workplace.

This is where CrewAI becomes so valuable. It's a framework that allows you to clearly define these roles, tasks, and communication channels. You don't have to build all of this logic yourself from scratch. The abstraction of `Agent` and `Task` allows you to think about system behavior rather than prompt mechanics.

But it's also important to understand that LLMs still have limitations. They don't have true memory unless you simulate it by feeding them previous context. They can still hallucinate or fabricate facts, especially when prompts are too vague or goals are too broad. They don't inherently validate their outputs. This is why tools and context management are so important. When you give an agent a goal and access to a tool—like web search or a data store—it can produce far more accurate and grounded responses. And when you use CrewAI to chain these agents together, you reduce the cognitive load on the LLM and improve the reliability of the whole system.

To close this section, here's a practical exercise you can try on your own. Build a three-agent system that performs a basic data pipeline:

One agent performs a search on a given topic using a web tool.

Another extracts named entities from that text using the LLM's reasoning.

A third agent formats the results into a structured JSON report.

By the time you complete it, you'll have a functional multi-agent workflow powered entirely by LLMs, coordinated through CrewAI, and structured in a way that's easy to maintain and extend. That's the power of embedding LLMs in multi-agent systems—they stop being just predictors of text and start behaving like intelligent collaborators.

Core Concepts of Agentic AI Systems

If you've worked with APIs, services, or even microservices before, then you already understand how modern software is often built around the idea of specialized components that each perform a specific function. What makes agentic systems different—and more powerful in the context of AI—is that each of these components isn't just a static unit of logic. Each one is built around a **goal**, it has the ability to reason, it can use tools, and it can interact with other agents to collaboratively complete tasks.

At the center of every agentic AI system is the **agent** itself. An agent is not a model. It uses a model—typically a large language model—as its core reasoning engine, but an agent is more than that. An agent is defined by a role, a purpose, some knowledge or instructions, and often a set of tools it can use to act on the world or gather information. This structure gives you more control over how the model behaves, what it's allowed to do, and how it fits into a larger workflow.

To understand how agents work in CrewAI, let's look at a basic agent definition:

```
from crewai import Agent
from langchain.chat_models import ChatOpenAI

agent = Agent(
    role="Technical Support Assistant",
```

```
    goal="Answer user questions accurately and
escalate complex issues when needed",
    backstory="You are a helpful and patient
technical support assistant specializing in
troubleshooting software issues.",
    llm=ChatOpenAI(temperature=0),
    verbose=True
)
```

This agent is now a complete entity. It's not just a model waiting for a prompt—it's a support agent with a purpose. It can be assigned tasks that it will approach in context with this role and goal in mind. Because of this design, you can build systems that are more predictable and aligned with user expectations. You're telling the model not only what you want it to do, but **why it exists**, and giving it a structured identity.

To make an agent useful, you need to give it something to do. In CrewAI, that something is called a **task**. A task is a structured instruction for the agent, designed to accomplish a specific objective. Think of it as the actual work that's being assigned. The task carries a description, an expected outcome, and the agent responsible for executing it.

Here's how you define one:

```
from crewai import Task

support_task = Task(
    description="Assist the user with resolving
their issue connecting to the database.",
    expected_output="A step-by-step response that
helps the user troubleshoot the connection issue.",
    agent=agent
)
```

Once you have a task assigned to an agent, you have the basic building blocks of a functional AI system. But things get really interesting when you bring in **tools**. A tool is any external capability that an agent can use as part of its reasoning. This might include web search, code execution, database querying, or even triggering HTTP endpoints.

For example, if your support agent needs to search for known issues or documentation online, you might attach a search tool like this:

```
from langchain.tools import DuckDuckGoSearchRun

search_tool = DuckDuckGoSearchRun()

agent.tools = [search_tool]
```

Now the agent doesn't just guess how to help—it can consult external knowledge in real time. This turns the model from a static predictor into an active participant in the task. You've moved from a single-shot generation to something closer to intelligent behavior.

In CrewAI, when you have multiple agents working together, each with their own goals and tools, you organize them into what's called a **crew**. The crew is the orchestrator. It holds the agents and tasks, and when executed, it coordinates the flow of execution—deciding which task goes to which agent, in what order, and how the outputs are passed along.

Let's see how this fits together:

```
from crewai import Crew

crew = Crew(
    agents=[agent],
    tasks=[support_task],
    verbose=True
)

crew_result = crew.run()
print(crew_result)
```

This structure becomes even more valuable when you introduce multiple agents and assign them different responsibilities. For instance, a **triage agent** might handle common cases, a **technical expert agent** might handle escalations, and a **reporting agent** could write summaries of resolved cases for analytics.

Here's where the concept of a **process handler** becomes important. This defines the coordination strategy for how agents work together. CrewAI offers predefined strategies like sequential execution, where tasks are performed one after another in order, and hierarchical execution, where one agent oversees others and delegates subtasks based on goals.

You don't need to use complex logic to start. CrewAI's default sequential process handler works well for most straightforward workflows. But if you want more control—say, routing based on agent responses, conditional branching, or task splitting—you can define a custom process handler. That gives you full programmatic control over how tasks are issued, repeated, or rerouted.

Here's a simplified example of two agents working sequentially in a research-writing workflow:

```
researcher = Agent(
    role="Research Analyst",
    goal="Find credible sources about AI trends in
healthcare",
    backstory="You are skilled at research and
summarization, especially in technology and
health.",
    tools=[search_tool],
    verbose=True
)

writer = Agent(
    role="Content Creator",
    goal="Write a blog post based on research data
provided by the analyst",
    backstory="You are a tech-savvy writer who
excels at producing concise, engaging content.",
    verbose=True
)

research_task = Task(
    description="Use web search to gather recent
developments in AI for healthcare.",
    expected_output="A bullet list of 3 to 5
developments, each with a source link.",
    agent=researcher
)
```

```python
write_task = Task(
    description="Take the research and write a 500-
word article on how AI is transforming
healthcare.",
    expected_output="A markdown-formatted blog post
suitable for a general audience.",
    agent=writer,
    context=[research_task]
)

crew = Crew(
    agents=[researcher, writer],
    tasks=[research_task, write_task],
    verbose=True
)

final_output = crew.run()
print(final_output)
```

In this scenario, each agent sticks to its expertise. The researcher finds the data. The writer creates the content. CrewAI handles the coordination. You're no longer writing a fragile sequence of prompts—you're building a modular, intelligent system composed of cooperating agents.

This modular design has significant benefits when you start thinking about production systems. It's easier to test individual components, swap out one agent for another, retry failed tasks, and scale horizontally. If one agent fails, you can handle that gracefully. If the workflow grows, you just define more agents and assign them tasks. And because each component is isolated but cooperative, you reduce coupling while increasing clarity and reusability.

When designing agentic systems, the key is to start thinking in terms of **goals, roles, and responsibilities**, not just outputs. Each agent should have a clearly defined purpose, the right tools to accomplish its tasks, and enough context to make decisions. CrewAI gives you the structure to enforce that without locking you into rigid workflows.

As you progress through this book, you'll use these core concepts—agents, tasks, tools, crews, and handlers—to build systems that are far more powerful and adaptable than anything a single prompt could achieve. These aren't just abstractions. They're practical building blocks that let you harness LLMs in a structured, reliable, and production-ready way.

Rise of Multi-Agent Coordination Frameworks

As language models became more capable, it didn't take long for developers to realize that a single prompt wasn't enough to build intelligent systems. It was clear that while an LLM could generate impressive responses, it struggled with complex workflows—especially those requiring memory, structured planning, or collaboration. Developers began searching for ways to give these models more structure, more continuity, and more autonomy—without reinventing the wheel for every new application.

That need gave birth to a new class of tools known as **multi-agent coordination frameworks**. These frameworks are designed to help developers define, manage, and orchestrate collections of AI agents that can work together to complete sophisticated tasks. They make it possible to move from building clever prompt scripts to architecting modular, cooperative systems of AI components that resemble distributed software.

The reason this shift happened so quickly is because the old way of working—manually chaining prompts, stitching responses together in scripts, and juggling context windows—was both fragile and exhausting. Developers wanted to build systems that felt like teams, where each agent handled a part of the job and the overall system behaved in a predictable, maintainable way.

Let me give you a practical example. Suppose you're building a customer success platform that automatically reviews support tickets, categorizes them by issue type, identifies accounts at risk, and drafts follow-up emails. If you try to solve this using a single prompt and a single model call, you'll end up writing a massive prompt full of context, edge cases, and expectations—all of which the model must handle in one go. That's not scalable or robust.

Instead, you could break this process into smaller parts:

One agent reads and classifies the support ticket.

A second agent checks the customer's history and flags high-risk accounts.

A third agent writes a tailored response using both the classification and customer context.

These agents can run sequentially or even in parallel, depending on your coordination strategy. But building this by hand—defining each message pass, context merge, and response parser—is time-consuming and error-prone. That's where frameworks come in. They manage the flow, memory, and execution while you focus on what the system is supposed to do.

Several coordination frameworks have emerged to solve this problem in slightly different ways, but most of them revolve around the same key needs: defining agents, assigning tasks, connecting those agents into a workflow, and managing their interactions.

Let's talk about how this plays out with **CrewAI**, because it addresses these needs in a particularly clean and developer-friendly way.

CrewAI doesn't try to hide everything behind abstraction. Instead, it gives you direct access to the components you care about—agents, tasks, tools, and crews—while handling the heavy lifting of context sharing, task assignment, and result flow. You don't have to design message protocols or write state machines. You declare what each agent is responsible for and how tasks are connected, and CrewAI does the coordination.

To show you what that looks like in code, let's build a lightweight coordination example using three agents:

A **TriagerAgent** that reads a support ticket and classifies it.

A **HistoryAgent** that pulls information about the customer.

A **ResponderAgent** that writes an email based on the classification and history.

Here's how you can define that workflow using CrewAI:

```
from crewai import Agent, Task, Crew

triager = Agent(
    role='Support Ticket Classifier',
    goal='Identify the category of a support
request and flag if urgent',
```

```python
    backstory='You specialize in categorizing and
triaging support tickets.',
    verbose=True
)

history_agent = Agent(
    role='Customer History Analyzer',
    goal='Review the customer's history and assess
risk or churn signals',
    backstory='You analyze behavior patterns and
past support tickets to determine customer
sentiment.',
    verbose=True
)

responder = Agent(
    role='Response Generator',
    goal='Write an empathetic and personalized
email response to the user',
    backstory='You write effective and polite
customer success emails with a human tone.',
    verbose=True
)

ticket_task = Task(
    description='Classify this support request:
"The software crashes every time I export a
report."',
    expected_output='A classification label such as
"Bug", "Feature Request", or "Usability Issue" with
an urgency flag.',
    agent=triager
)

history_task = Task(
    description='Given the customer's past
interactions, summarize their engagement level and
list any red flags.',
    expected_output='A paragraph describing
customer status and warning signs.',
    agent=history_agent
)
```

```
response_task = Task(
    description='Based on the classification and
customer history, write an empathetic support email
that acknowledges the issue and outlines next
steps.',
    expected_output='A short, professional email
that can be sent to the customer.',
    agent=responder,
    context=[ticket_task, history_task]
)

crew = Crew(
    agents=[triager, history_agent, responder],
    tasks=[ticket_task, history_task,
response_task],
    verbose=True
)

output = crew.run()
print(output)
```

This example demonstrates a coordinated multi-agent system built entirely in Python using CrewAI. Each agent has a specific function, each task is clearly defined, and the coordination between them is handled automatically. There is no need to manually pass variables, construct shared prompts, or stitch together responses—CrewAI manages all that behind the scenes. This makes your system both scalable and easier to maintain over time.

What makes this kind of coordination particularly valuable is that it closely mirrors how humans work in structured teams. No one person handles the entire pipeline. Instead, individuals specialize, and their outputs feed into each other's work. The software world has long known the benefits of modular design—now, with coordination frameworks like CrewAI, we're applying that same principle to AI behavior.

It's also worth noting that other frameworks, such as LangChain Agents or AutoGen, offer similar agent coordination features, but with slightly different philosophies. LangChain often leans toward chains of prompts and tools, while AutoGen focuses on dialogue-based agent collaboration. Both are powerful, and each has its use cases. But CrewAI tends to be more approachable for structured workflows, especially when your goal is to assign agents to discrete tasks and let them pass work forward as part of a pipeline.

Coordination frameworks are still evolving quickly, but the pattern is here to stay. As AI use becomes more complex—spanning tasks like customer onboarding, product generation, document analysis, and dynamic planning— it becomes less about making a single model smarter and more about orchestrating multiple specialized agents in a thoughtful way. That's what CrewAI and similar frameworks are enabling: not smarter models, but smarter systems.

Where CrewAI Fits in the AI Landscape

If you've been keeping an eye on how AI tooling has evolved recently, you've probably noticed that we've moved beyond standalone prompts and one-off model calls. More developers are building intelligent systems that need structure, collaboration, and coordination—especially when those systems are expected to run reliably, not just experiment in a notebook.

That's where CrewAI stands out.

CrewAI is designed specifically for developers who want to build **multi-agent systems** without having to design their own coordination logic or build custom prompt-passing infrastructure. It's not a research playground or a generalized AI interface. It's a developer-focused framework that treats agents as composable, predictable units of work and gives you control over how they operate within a structured workflow.

To understand where CrewAI fits into the broader ecosystem, it helps to compare what you'd have to do **without** a framework like this.

If you wanted to build a multi-agent pipeline manually, you'd have to write the glue code for prompt generation, manage intermediate outputs, pass structured results between agents, maintain histories, and ensure agents stay within their defined scope. That alone could mean writing hundreds of lines of code just to get basic coordination working—and it becomes harder to test, debug, or modify as the complexity grows.

CrewAI removes that burden by providing a clear structure:

You define **agents**, each with a role, a goal, a backstory, and optional tools.

You define **tasks** that those agents will perform, with inputs and expected outputs.

You group them into a **crew**, and CrewAI manages the execution—handling the order, data flow, and agent reasoning context.

This model gives you something that other frameworks often obscure: **clarity**.

For example, let's say you're building a technical documentation assistant. You want one agent to extract technical details from a codebase, another to generate human-readable explanations, and a third to clean up and format the output for publishing. This is a real-world scenario, especially for internal tools used by developer experience teams.

Here's how you could structure that in CrewAI without needing to build coordination logic from scratch:

```
from crewai import Agent, Task, Crew

extractor = Agent(
    role='Codebase Analyzer',
    goal='Extract key components and function
descriptions from source code',
    backstory='You specialize in understanding
software structure and identifying important
patterns.',
    verbose=True
)

explainer = Agent(
    role='Technical Explainer',
    goal='Convert technical code summaries into
clear explanations for readers',
    backstory='You're experienced in translating
software logic into human-friendly language.',
    verbose=True
)

formatter = Agent(
    role='Documentation Formatter',
    goal='Prepare technical content for publishing
in Markdown with proper structure and formatting',
```

```python
    backstory='You have deep familiarity with
developer documentation standards and formatting
tools.',
    verbose=True
)

analyze_task = Task(
    description='Analyze this Python file and
summarize the main functions and classes:
./my_project/utils/data_loader.py',
    expected_output='A list of functions and
classes with brief descriptions.',
    agent=extractor
)

explain_task = Task(
    description='Take the summaries from the code
analyzer and generate human-readable explanations
for each item.',
    expected_output='A sectioned explanation in
natural language, suitable for technical
documentation.',
    agent=explainer,
    context=[analyze_task]
)

format_task = Task(
    description='Format the explanations into
Markdown with appropriate headers and spacing.',
    expected_output='Well-structured Markdown text
ready to be published on GitHub or a docs site.',
    agent=formatter,
    context=[explain_task]
)

crew = Crew(
    agents=[extractor, explainer, formatter],
    tasks=[analyze_task, explain_task,
format_task],
    verbose=True
)
```

```
result = crew.run()
print(result)
```

There's nothing magical here. No hidden abstraction layers. You're writing code that directly reflects the system architecture. You can look at this and immediately understand which agent is doing what, how tasks are structured, and how outputs are passed between them. This is especially important for production systems, where maintainability, traceability, and testability matter.

When you compare this to other multi-agent tools, such as LangChain's agent executor or Microsoft's AutoGen, the distinction becomes clearer. Those frameworks often lean into abstraction: they prioritize dynamic behavior, conversational agents, or chainable tool calling, which can be powerful but less predictable. That might be ideal for prototyping or AI research, but in real-world applications, where workflows are long-running or require consistency, you need something you can test, reason about, and version.

CrewAI takes a more pragmatic approach. It's declarative where you want structure and flexible where you want control. That's why it fits so naturally into production pipelines. You can wrap each crew as a callable service, expose it through a REST API, or deploy it as a microservice inside a larger application.

Let me give you another real-world context where CrewAI shines: internal operations automation.

Suppose your team is using AI to streamline onboarding for new hires. You want an agent to gather relevant documentation, another to personalize an onboarding email based on role and department, and a third to schedule a welcome session and notify the relevant team lead. You can model each step as a task and assign it to a dedicated agent. And with CrewAI, you don't have to code the control flow from scratch or worry about state synchronization. You define the structure once, and then run it as often as needed.

This is what makes CrewAI not just useful—but **reliable**.

You're not building black boxes. You're building modular, observable, understandable AI systems. That's exactly what's needed as organizations move from experimenting with AI to actually **depending** on it. Tools that work for demos often fail under pressure. CrewAI is designed for developers who want confidence in how their systems behave—not just when things go right, but also when something fails, stalls, or needs to scale.

In this broader landscape of AI development, CrewAI positions itself as a structured, developer-friendly tool for building **coordinated intelligent systems**, not just prompting engines. It gives you the freedom to define what intelligence should look like in your application—and then enforces that structure in a way that's easy to reason about, extend, and maintain.

Chapter 2: Setting Up the CrewAI Environment

Before you can build agent systems with CrewAI, you need to get your development environment ready. This chapter is all about laying that foundation. We'll walk through installing CrewAI and its dependencies, connecting to your preferred language model provider (like OpenAI), organizing your files in a clean and maintainable way, and writing your first working two-agent crew. By the time you finish, you'll have a project up and running, and a clear understanding of how things are wired together behind the scenes.

This isn't just about getting something to work once—it's about building a stable foundation that's easy to extend, maintain, and share as your projects grow more advanced.

Installing CrewAI and Dependencies

Before you can build anything meaningful with CrewAI, you'll need to get your development environment set up correctly. Installing CrewAI is straightforward, but since it's designed to integrate with language models, tools, and orchestration logic, there are a few moving parts to pay attention to. Getting this right from the beginning will save you a lot of time later on.

First, let's talk about Python. CrewAI is written in Python and depends on features from modern Python versions, so you should be using **Python 3.9 or later**. If you're unsure what version you have installed, you can check by running:

```
python --version
```

or

```
python3 --version
```

If your version is lower than 3.9, you'll need to upgrade Python before continuing. On macOS or Linux, it's often easiest to install via Homebrew or `pyenv`. On Windows, you can download the latest installer from the official Python site.

Once you've confirmed your Python version, the next step is to create an **isolated virtual environment**. This helps you avoid version conflicts between projects and keeps everything tidy. Here's how to do that:

```
python3 -m venv crewai-env
```

Now activate the virtual environment:

On macOS and Linux:

```
source crewai-env/bin/activate
```

On Windows:

```
crewai-env\Scripts\activate
```

When your virtual environment is active, your terminal prompt will usually show the environment name, and any packages you install will be confined to this environment.

With that in place, you're ready to install **CrewAI**. CrewAI is available on PyPI, which means you can install it directly using `pip`:

```
pip install crewai
```

This will pull in CrewAI and its dependencies, including its core dependency: **LangChain**. LangChain handles a lot of the underlying logic for connecting to language models, calling tools, and managing prompts. You don't need to interact with LangChain directly to use CrewAI, but it's doing a lot of the heavy lifting behind the scenes.

To use most real-world language models, especially OpenAI models like GPT-4 or GPT-3.5-turbo, you'll also need to install OpenAI's Python SDK:

```
pip install openai
```

This allows CrewAI to send your agent prompts to OpenAI and retrieve completions.

While you're at it, it's good practice to also install the **python-dotenv** package. This helps you manage your API keys and environment variables without hardcoding secrets into your scripts:

```
pip install python-dotenv
```

You now have the core packages you need to build multi-agent systems using CrewAI. If you want to verify everything is installed correctly, you can run a quick test. Open a Python shell or create a new script and type the following:

```
from crewai import Agent
print("CrewAI is installed and ready.")
```

If you see no errors, you're in great shape.

At this point, you've got the core framework in place, but you still need to connect it to an actual LLM provider so the agents can reason, generate content, and interact intelligently. Most developers start with OpenAI, and for good reason: GPT-4 and GPT-3.5 are both powerful, consistent, and easy to access.

To use OpenAI, you'll need to obtain an API key. Log in to your account at platform.openai.com, and create a new secret key under your account settings. Copy this key and save it in a file called .env at the root of your project:

```
OPENAI_API_KEY=sk-XXXXXXXXXXXXXXXXXXXXXXXXXXXXXXXXXXXXXXXXXXXX
```

Make sure you never check this .env file into version control. It should always be listed in your .gitignore file.

In your Python script, load the environment variables using load_dotenv() before using any models:

```
from dotenv import load_dotenv
load_dotenv()
```

To initialize the actual model, CrewAI relies on LangChain's model wrappers. You can create an instance of OpenAI's chat model like this:

```
from langchain.chat_models import ChatOpenAI

llm = ChatOpenAI(model_name="gpt-4",
temperature=0.3)
```

This model object can now be passed into any CrewAI agent, giving it the ability to perform reasoning and generation.

Let's test the full setup with a simple echo agent, just to confirm everything is working:

```
from dotenv import load_dotenv
from langchain.chat_models import ChatOpenAI
from crewai import Agent, Task, Crew

load_dotenv()

llm = ChatOpenAI(model_name="gpt-4", temperature=0)

agent = Agent(
    role="Echo Bot",
    goal="Repeat back anything the user says",
    backstory="You are a polite assistant who
echoes messages.",
    llm=llm,
    verbose=True
)

task = Task(
    description="Repeat the phrase: 'Hello,
CrewAI!'",
    expected_output="Hello, CrewAI!",
    agent=agent
)

crew = Crew(
    agents=[agent],
    tasks=[task],
    verbose=True
)

output = crew.run()
print(output)
```

When you run this script, your terminal should output a message that looks like it was generated by a polite assistant repeating your phrase. This confirms that your environment, API connection, and base CrewAI configuration are all functioning properly.

At this point, you're ready to start building real agents and structured crews. In the next section, we'll configure your LLM backends more robustly and discuss how to support different providers beyond OpenAI—like Anthropic or local models—if needed. But for now, your CrewAI development environment is fully operational.

Setting Up OpenAI or LLM Backends

To make any CrewAI agent useful, you need to connect it to a language model that can handle its reasoning, generate its responses, and interpret the tasks it's assigned. CrewAI itself doesn't include a model. Instead, it relies on integrations with third-party providers like OpenAI, Anthropic, Cohere, and others via the LangChain ecosystem.

By far, the most common and stable choice today is OpenAI's GPT-4 or GPT-3.5 models. These models are well-supported, performant, and extremely capable in multi-agent settings. They handle context well, respond consistently, and are easy to access with a simple API key.

Let's walk through the setup process for OpenAI step by step, and I'll explain exactly what's happening along the way.

Start by signing in to your account at platform.openai.com. Once you're logged in, click your avatar in the top right corner, go to **API keys,** and click **Create new secret key**. This gives you a key that will look something like:

`sk-XXXXXXXXXXXXXXXXXXXXXXXXXXXXXXXXXXXXXXXXXXXX`

Treat this key like a password. You don't want to paste it into scripts or upload it to GitHub. Instead, save it in a `.env` file at the root of your project directory:

`OPENAI_API_KEY=sk-XXXXXXXXXXXXXXXXXXXXXXXXXXXXXXXXXXXXXXXXXXXX`

This file will store sensitive environment variables, and we'll use `python-dotenv` to load them into your Python application automatically.

Now let's write the Python code that connects to OpenAI.

First, load the environment variables from your `.env` file:

```
from dotenv import load_dotenv
load_dotenv()
```

Next, import the OpenAI-compatible language model wrapper from LangChain. CrewAI uses these wrappers to connect your agents to the actual model backend:

```
from langchain.chat_models import ChatOpenAI
```

Now you can instantiate the LLM object with your desired configuration:

```
llm = ChatOpenAI(
    model_name="gpt-4",           # You can use "gpt-
3.5-turbo" for a faster, cheaper option
    temperature=0.3,              # Lower values mean
more deterministic responses
    max_tokens=1024               # Optional: adjust
based on task needs
)
```

At this point, `llm` is a fully configured instance that can be passed into any CrewAI agent. Let's build a minimal agent to verify that everything's wired up correctly:

```
from crewai import Agent, Task, Crew

agent = Agent(
    role="Echo Bot",
    goal="Repeat whatever is requested, with a
helpful tone",
    backstory="You are a polite assistant trained
to echo messages for debugging purposes.",
    llm=llm,
    verbose=True
)

task = Task(
    description="Repeat the phrase: 'Welcome to
CrewAI!'",
    expected_output="Welcome to CrewAI!",
    agent=agent
)

crew = Crew(
    agents=[agent],
    tasks=[task],
    verbose=True
)

output = crew.run()
```

```
print(output)
```

Run this file in your terminal. If everything is working, you'll see CrewAI delegate the task to the agent, and the agent will return a polite echo of the phrase. If the model fails to respond or the script exits with an error like `openai.error.AuthenticationError`, then double-check your `.env` file and make sure it's being loaded at runtime.

If your key is valid but you're getting timeout errors or rate limits, it's possible your account doesn't have access to GPT-4 yet—or you're hitting usage caps. You can change to GPT-3.5 like this:

```
llm = ChatOpenAI(model_name="gpt-3.5-turbo",
temperature=0.3)
```

Both models work seamlessly with CrewAI, and you can swap them based on the task's complexity and performance needs. GPT-4 is better for reasoning-heavy workflows, while GPT-3.5 is excellent for faster, lower-cost tasks like formatting, basic classification, or summarization.

Now, if you'd rather not use OpenAI or want to prepare for flexibility later, CrewAI can work with any LLM supported by LangChain. That includes models like Claude from Anthropic, Cohere's command models, Hugging Face-hosted endpoints, or even local models via Llama.cpp or Ollama.

For example, to use Anthropic's Claude, you would change the import and instantiation like this:

```
from langchain.chat_models import ChatAnthropic

llm = ChatAnthropic(
    model="claude-2.1",
    temperature=0.2,
    max_tokens_to_sample=1024
)
```

You'd then store your Anthropic API key in the `.env` file as:

ANTHROPIC_API_KEY=your-anthropic-key-here

LangChain and CrewAI will handle the authentication as long as the key is correctly loaded into the environment.

When using local models such as Llama 2 or Mistral, things get more complex. You'll need to run the model server yourself (using something like `llama-cpp-python`, `text-generation-webui`, or `Ollama`), and you'll integrate via LangChain's `ChatOpenAI`, `ChatCTransformers`, or a custom wrapper. That's outside the scope of initial development, but completely possible once you've stabilized your architecture.

For now, I recommend starting with OpenAI or Anthropic because the setup is fast, the results are strong, and they integrate cleanly with CrewAI's agent-task structure.

Once your backend is in place, everything else builds on top of that. Every agent you create, every task you assign, and every tool you connect will eventually route through the language model you've set up here. So it's important to test it early, confirm that your completions are returning correctly, and make sure your API usage fits your budget and capacity needs.

As we move forward into more advanced parts of the framework, you'll have the option to configure fallback models, adjust temperature settings dynamically per task, or even assign different LLMs to different agents in the same crew. But all of that starts with this basic setup.

At this point, your environment should be fully equipped to run CrewAI agents with OpenAI or any other LangChain-supported model. In the next section, I'll show you how to structure your files and folders for a clean and maintainable CrewAI project—something you'll appreciate once your system grows beyond a couple of agents and a single script.

Folder Structure and Project Layout

When you start a small script using CrewAI—maybe a single agent performing one task—it might be tempting to throw everything into a single file and call it a day. And for quick experiments, that's fine. But as soon as you introduce multiple agents, more than one task, or anything resembling a reusable pipeline, you'll quickly find yourself stuck in a tangle of copy-pasted code, long function bodies, and growing confusion over what lives where.

Setting up a clean folder structure at the beginning pays off fast. It helps you stay organized, share your work with teammates, and debug problems without hunting through hundreds of lines of nested logic. It also makes it easier to test components independently—like running one agent's logic in isolation or swapping out a tool without affecting your whole project.

Let's take the practical route and walk through a structure that scales cleanly as your project evolves. Start by creating a root folder for your project—something like `ai-team-assistant` or `crewai-pipeline`.

Inside that folder, you'll want to separate your agents, tasks, tools, and orchestration logic into their own Python modules. This doesn't require any advanced Python packaging knowledge—it just means grouping related code into separate files and folders so each piece stays modular.

Here's how the structure might look on your machine:

```
crewai-pipeline/
├── agents/
│   ├── researcher.py
│   └── writer.py
├── tasks/
│   ├── research_task.py
│   └── write_task.py
├── tools/
│   └── web_search.py
├── crews/
│   └── blog_creator.py
├── main.py
├── .env
├── requirements.txt
└── README.md
```

Let's break that structure down in practical terms.

Your `agents/` folder contains each agent definition in its own file. For instance, `researcher.py` might contain a `ResearcherAgent` class or function that returns a configured CrewAI agent object. That way, you can reuse the same agent in multiple crews, or replace it later without rewriting every file where it's used.

Here's what `agents/researcher.py` might contain:

```python
from crewai import Agent
from langchain.chat_models import ChatOpenAI
from langchain.tools import DuckDuckGoSearchRun

llm = ChatOpenAI(model_name="gpt-4",
temperature=0.5)
search_tool = DuckDuckGoSearchRun()

def get_researcher_agent():
    return Agent(
        role="AI Researcher",
        goal="Identify and summarize important news
in AI",
        backstory="You are an experienced
researcher who stays current with AI
developments.",
        tools=[search_tool],
        llm=llm,
        verbose=True
    )
```

Notice that this returns a **function** instead of instantiating the agent in the global scope. That's intentional. It gives you flexibility. You can import this function wherever you need it, and it won't execute until called. This becomes especially useful later when testing or creating multiple crews.

Your `tasks/` folder follows a similar pattern. Each file defines one task that you'll assign to an agent. Here's an example from `tasks/research_task.py`:

```python
from crewai import Task
from agents.researcher import get_researcher_agent

def get_research_task():
    return Task(
```

```
        description="Use web search to find the
latest three developments in artificial
intelligence and summarize them.",
        expected_output="A list of three key
developments, each with a short description and a
source link.",
        agent=get_researcher_agent()
    )
```

This makes your tasks reusable and keeps your main orchestration logic clean.

In the tools/ folder, you can define custom tools when the built-in ones aren't enough. For example, if you need to query an internal database or hit a private API, you can wrap that functionality in a LangChain-compatible tool and include it in the agent's configuration.

Your crews/ folder is where the coordination logic lives. Think of it as the blueprint for assembling agents and tasks into a functional workflow. Here's an example from crews/blog_creator.py:

```
from crewai import Crew
from tasks.research_task import get_research_task
from tasks.write_task import get_write_task
from agents.writer import get_writer_agent
from agents.researcher import get_researcher_agent

def get_blog_creator_crew():
    return Crew(
        agents=[get_researcher_agent(),
get_writer_agent()],
        tasks=[get_research_task(),
get_write_task()],
        verbose=True
    )
```

This file doesn't handle any logic itself—it just assembles the pieces and returns a configured crew. That makes it very easy to manage and test.

Then, in your main.py, you can bring everything together with very little code:

```
from crews.blog_creator import
get_blog_creator_crew
```

```
from dotenv import load_dotenv

load_dotenv()

if __name__ == "__main__":
    crew = get_blog_creator_crew()
    result = crew.run()
    print(result)
```

Now your `main.py` stays readable and short, while the complexity is abstracted into clearly named modules that you can navigate and modify independently. If your system grows to support multiple workflows—for example, blog generation, trend analysis, or newsletter creation—you can add more files to `crews/` and follow the same pattern without any confusion.

This modular structure also plays nicely with version control. If something breaks, you'll be able to trace the problem to a specific agent or task file, rather than scanning through one massive script. And if you start working with a team, each person can own different parts of the system without stepping on each other's work.

It's also easier to write unit tests when your logic is separated into small, testable components. You can import one agent or task at a time and validate that it behaves as expected under different conditions. That might not seem urgent right now, but as your system starts automating more critical work, you'll want to have that confidence built in.

Lastly, don't forget to maintain your `requirements.txt` file as you add dependencies. After installing or updating packages, run:

pip freeze > requirements.txt

This ensures your environment is reproducible across machines or deployment servers.

With this structure in place, you're ready to build CrewAI projects that are clean, testable, and easy to expand. Your next step is to create your first working script with two cooperating agents, which will show you how these parts come together in a complete workflow.

Hello Crew

Now that you've got your environment set up, your API key in place, and your project structure ready, it's time to build your first working multi-agent script. This won't just be an abstract test or a toy example. It will be a real CrewAI-powered workflow with two agents, each with their own distinct role, working together to accomplish a task from start to finish.

We'll start with a simple but meaningful scenario: creating a blog article based on recent developments in artificial intelligence. One agent will act as a researcher, using a web search tool to gather information. The other agent will take that research and generate a blog post.

You'll see how CrewAI helps you define clear responsibilities for each agent, assign tasks, and pass information between them without writing any complex orchestration code.

Before writing the final script, make sure you've installed the required packages in your virtual environment:

pip install crewai openai langchain python-dotenv

Also, make sure you have the OpenAI API key saved in a .env file at the root of your project like this:

**OPENAI_API_KEY=sk-
xxxxxxxxxxxxxxxxxxxxxxxxxxxxxxxxxxxxxxxxxxxx**

Let's now walk through the complete script together. You can place all this into a file named main.py at the root of your project folder.

```python
# main.py

from dotenv import load_dotenv
from langchain.chat_models import ChatOpenAI
from langchain.tools import DuckDuckGoSearchRun
from crewai import Agent, Task, Crew

# Load your environment variables
load_dotenv()

# Set up the language model
```

```python
llm = ChatOpenAI(
    model_name="gpt-4",   # You can use gpt-3.5-
turbo for faster responses
    temperature=0.3
)

# Set up a web search tool
search_tool = DuckDuckGoSearchRun()

# Define the first agent: the Researcher
researcher = Agent(
    role="AI Research Specialist",
    goal="Find and summarize the top three recent
advancements in AI",
    backstory="You are an expert in tracking AI
innovation and breakthroughs across academic and
industry news.",
    tools=[search_tool],
    llm=llm,
    verbose=True
)

# Define the second agent: the Writer
writer = Agent(
    role="Technical Content Writer",
    goal="Generate a blog post from the research
findings",
    backstory="You are a professional writer who
explains complex topics in a way that is accessible
to a broad audience.",
    llm=llm,
    verbose=True
)

# Create a task for the Researcher
research_task = Task(
    description=(
        "Use your web search capabilities to
identify and summarize the top three most recent
advancements "
```

```python
        "in artificial intelligence from trusted
sources such as Google AI, OpenAI, DeepMind, or
academic publications."
    ),
    expected_output=(
        "A list of three developments, each with a
one-paragraph summary and a source link."
    ),
    agent=researcher
)

# Create a task for the Writer
write_task = Task(
    description=(
        "Using the research findings, write a 500-
word blog post titled 'The Latest Breakthroughs in
AI You Should Know About'. "
        "Format it in Markdown with appropriate
headers and structure. The tone should be
informative and clear."
    ),
    expected_output=(
        "A well-structured Markdown blog post with
an introduction, three key sections, and a
conclusion."
    ),
    agent=writer,
    context=[research_task]  # This links the
Writer's input to the Researcher's output
)

# Assemble the crew
crew = Crew(
    agents=[researcher, writer],
    tasks=[research_task, write_task],
    verbose=True
)

# Run the crew
result = crew.run()

# Display the result
```

```
print("\n\n===== Final Output =====\n\n")
print(result)
```

When you run this file with `python main.py`, you're running a fully functional multi-agent workflow:

The **researcher** agent executes a web search using DuckDuckGo, interprets the results, and returns structured summaries of recent developments in AI.

The **writer** agent takes those summaries, applies its understanding of how to structure informative content, and generates a complete Markdown-formatted blog post.

This process is entirely automatic. You didn't have to hard-code any data flow or format parsing. You simply defined what each agent should do, described the task clearly, and connected them through the `context` parameter in the second task.

Let's pause to highlight what just happened here, because it's a big shift in how you may be used to working with language models.

You didn't send a prompt and wait for a single response. You built a **workflow** using two autonomous agents, each with their own role, reasoning model, and tool access. The structure you created didn't just run once—it can be reused across different topics, or even adapted to entirely different domains like financial analysis, technical documentation, or customer support automation.

You can also test each agent individually. For example, if you want to validate the research agent's accuracy, you can run just the first task and review its output. If the blog content doesn't read well, you can tune the writer agent's prompt or replace its LLM backend with a faster or more creative model.

The flexibility here comes from the way CrewAI models **people-like roles and workflows**. It doesn't abstract away the complexity with hidden chains—it lets you build logical, modular systems that reflect how work actually happens.

Before moving on to more advanced orchestration and performance topics, you should spend some time experimenting with this structure. Try changing the topic from "artificial intelligence" to "quantum computing" or "climate tech." You'll see that with no code changes—only different task instructions—your agents will still coordinate effectively to complete the new task.

You've now written your first two-agent crew. It's working, it's reusable, and it's a real example of how multi-agent systems can perform meaningful, multi-step tasks with minimal overhead.

Troubleshooting and Versioning

No matter how clean your setup is, you're going to run into issues from time to time—especially when you're dealing with external APIs, evolving open-source libraries, or agent workflows that depend on consistent structure and context passing. This section is here to help you identify what's going wrong and fix it, without frustration or guesswork. You'll also learn how to lock your environment versions to avoid unexpected behavior as your project matures.

Let's start with the most common issue: **authentication errors** when connecting to a language model provider.

If you run your CrewAI script and get an error like `openai.error.AuthenticationError: No API key provided`, it means the model wrapper couldn't find your OpenAI key in the environment. This usually comes down to either a missing `.env` file or a failure to load it properly in your script.

Here's how to verify the basics step by step:

First, check that your `.env` file is in the root of your project and that it looks exactly like this (no quotes, no spaces around the equals sign):

OPENAI_API_KEY=sk-
xxxxxxxxxxxxxxxxxxxxxxxxxxxxxxxxxxxxxxxxxxx

Second, confirm you're calling `load_dotenv()` before initializing any model or agent that relies on the API key:

```
from dotenv import load_dotenv
load_dotenv()
```

This line must appear **before** any code that uses `ChatOpenAI()` or accesses the `os.environ` dictionary.

To verify that the environment variable is actually being loaded, add a quick print check right after calling `load_dotenv()`:

```
import os
print("OpenAI Key Loaded:",
os.getenv("OPENAI_API_KEY"))
```

If this prints `None`, it means your key isn't being loaded. You may need to check your file naming (ensure it's `.env`, not `.env.txt`) or make sure it's in the same directory where you're running your script.

If your API key is loaded correctly but your calls are timing out, failing intermittently, or returning rate-limit errors, it's likely a capacity issue. The GPT-4 model, in particular, has tighter rate limits and can return errors if too many requests are sent in a short time. When that happens, consider switching temporarily to GPT-3.5 for testing:

llm = ChatOpenAI(model_name="gpt-3.5-turbo", temperature=0.3)

This model is faster and has more relaxed usage limits. You can return to GPT-4 later when your workflow is stabilized.

Another common issue is **tool integration failure**, especially if you're using third-party tools like `DuckDuckGoSearchRun`. If you define a tool in your agent but get errors about function execution, the problem usually stems from either a missing dependency or an outdated version of LangChain.

Start by making sure the required package is installed:

pip install duckduckgo-search

If that's already in place, the next step is to verify that your tool is correctly initialized and passed to the agent. Don't define tools outside of the agent's constructor unless you're assigning them explicitly afterward.

```
from langchain.tools import DuckDuckGoSearchRun
search_tool = DuckDuckGoSearchRun()

agent = Agent(
    role="Web Researcher",
    goal="Use web search to find recent AI trends",
```

```
    tools=[search_tool],
    llm=llm,
    verbose=True
)
```

If the tool executes but returns empty or unrelated results, that may not be a bug—it may just be the nature of the search tool. DuckDuckGo is fast but doesn't always return highly relevant academic or technical sources. For high-precision domains, consider creating your own tool using a focused API or curated knowledge base.

In multi-agent workflows, **context errors** are another issue you may run into. When you pass the output of one task into another using the `context` parameter, you must make sure the first task completes successfully and produces structured output that the second agent can understand. If your second agent gets confused, fails to respond, or generates irrelevant text, the problem is often in the formatting or clarity of the first agent's output.

To fix that, go back to the `expected_output` of the first task and make it more specific. Tell the agent exactly what kind of output you expect—bullet points, summaries, JSON, or Markdown—and define the format clearly.

```
expected_output=(
    "A list of exactly three AI developments. Each
should include: "
    "1) a short description, 2) the source link,
and 3) a brief impact statement."
)
```

Structured outputs reduce ambiguity and give downstream agents something to work with. You can also insert formatting validation if needed, by writing a small parser that checks the output between tasks before passing it on.

Once your system is working smoothly, it's time to prevent it from breaking in the future. That's where **versioning** becomes critical. CrewAI and LangChain are both under active development, and changes to internal APIs or dependency behavior can silently break your project if you update without realizing what's changed.

To protect yourself, use `pip freeze` to snapshot your environment:

```
pip freeze > requirements.txt
```

Then open `requirements.txt` and pin the versions you know are stable. For example:

```
crewai==0.20.2
```

```
openai==1.13.3
```

```
langchain==0.1.8
```

```
python-dotenv==1.0.1
```

This ensures that every time you or a teammate installs your project—even on a new machine—you'll get the exact same versions that you tested with.

If you use Git, make sure your `.env` file is excluded using `.gitignore`. But include your `requirements.txt`, `main.py`, and folder structure so the project can be cloned, set up, and run without extra steps.

From time to time, when you do want to upgrade packages to benefit from new features, do it in a separate branch or test environment. Don't blindly update everything with `pip install --upgrade` unless you're prepared to retest all workflows.

CrewAI is built on top of several moving parts—Python, LangChain, OpenAI, and any third-party tools you include. Managing versions carefully is the only way to guarantee reliability and avoid introducing problems as your system grows.

If you're sharing your project with others or preparing it for deployment, it's also smart to add a setup script or `Makefile` that installs dependencies and loads environment variables in a reproducible way. This extra step can prevent countless issues for you and your team.

By addressing configuration errors, dependency drift, and task structure issues early, you set yourself up for a much smoother development process. You're not just solving individual bugs—you're learning to build agent systems that are stable, reliable, and production-ready.

Chapter 3: Anatomy of an Agent

If you've been following along, you now have a working environment, a clean project structure, and your first multi-agent script running with CrewAI. Now it's time to take a closer look at what an agent actually is—how it's defined, what it can do, and how to design agents that are intelligent, consistent, and reusable.

Agents are the core of any CrewAI system. Every agent is an independent unit of reasoning and behavior, with its own role, goal, tools, and logic. When you build agents thoughtfully, the rest of your system becomes easier to scale and maintain. This chapter will show you exactly how to do that.

What Makes an Agent in CrewAI

When you're working with CrewAI, the most important unit in the entire system is the **agent**. Every task, every tool, every decision ultimately routes through one or more agents. So understanding what makes an agent—not just syntactically valid, but well-designed—is essential if you want to build intelligent and reliable systems.

In CrewAI, an agent isn't just a thin wrapper around a language model like GPT-4 or Claude. It's a structured component that you define explicitly with a role, a goal, a backstory, and optionally some tools. It can also be connected to a memory system or specialized logic if your use case demands it. That means when you define an agent, you're not just setting up how it talks— you're shaping its behavior, its tone, and even the way it reasons through tasks.

Let me show you what a real agent looks like in code, and then we'll break down every part of it.

```
from crewai import Agent
from langchain.chat_models import ChatOpenAI

llm = ChatOpenAI(model_name="gpt-4",
temperature=0.3)

support_agent = Agent(
    role="Technical Support Representative",
    goal="Help customers troubleshoot issues with
the CrewAI platform and guide them to a solution",
```

```
    backstory="You are a friendly and experienced
support representative who knows the CrewAI system
inside and out. You aim to be helpful, clear, and
reassuring.",
    llm=llm,
    verbose=True
)
```

Let's break this down piece by piece.

First, you're importing the `Agent` class from `crewai`, and you're using `ChatOpenAI` from `langchain.chat_models` to access OpenAI's GPT-based chat models. That `llm` instance is what the agent uses internally to generate its responses. You can configure it with a temperature, model name, and other parameters based on how creative or deterministic you want it to be.

Now look at the arguments passed into the `Agent` constructor:

`role`: This tells the agent who it's supposed to be. It's not just decorative. CrewAI includes the role in the prompt that is sent to the LLM, which heavily influences how the model responds. For example, a "Customer Support Representative" is going to speak very differently than a "Data Privacy Auditor" or a "Medical Research Analyst."

`goal`: This is the primary objective the agent is trying to accomplish—regardless of the specific task it's assigned. If you give an agent a task that says "Summarize this document," but its goal is "Critically assess documents for bias and misinformation," it will bring that lens to the summary. Goals act like a compass.

`backstory`: This is where you can shape the agent's tone, depth of knowledge, or background assumptions. While this isn't strictly required, it's extremely useful when you want consistent tone, deeper reasoning, or domain specificity. For example, if you're building a legal advisor agent, the backstory might include their familiarity with contract law or regulatory compliance.

`llm`: This is the language model that powers the agent. It could be GPT-4, GPT-3.5, Claude, or any other LangChain-compatible model. Every time the agent is invoked to complete a task, this model will be used under the hood.

verbose: When set to `True`, this allows the system to print detailed logs of what the agent is doing, which is incredibly helpful during development and debugging.

At this point, you have a fully defined agent. But that doesn't mean it's doing anything yet. An agent only acts when it's assigned a task through CrewAI's `Task` class. The power of the agent lies in how it interprets that task through the lens of its role and goal.

Let's see how that works in a minimal working example:

```python
from crewai import Task, Crew

task = Task(
    description="Assist a user who is unable to
export reports from CrewAI to PDF. Provide a clear
step-by-step solution or redirect them to the
correct documentation.",
    expected_output="A helpful response that solves
the issue or points the user to the appropriate
help resource.",
    agent=support_agent
)

crew = Crew(
    agents=[support_agent],
    tasks=[task],
    verbose=True
)

result = crew.run()
print(result)
```

In this example, you created a task and assigned it to the `support_agent`. That agent now processes the task using its internal LLM, guided by its role, goal, and backstory. It will generate a response that is aligned with those attributes.

Now, here's where things get more interesting. You could give the same task to a different agent—say, one with a more technical engineering role—and you'd get a completely different response. Maybe more detailed, more focused on debugging logs, or more direct in tone. This variability is a feature. It lets you build workflows where different agents bring different perspectives to the same data or input.

You're not just sending prompts anymore. You're building a reasoning pipeline with specialized participants.

If you want to expand what an agent can do, you can also give it tools—functions or APIs it can call during its reasoning. For example, you might give your support agent access to a documentation search tool so it can reference help pages. You'll see how to do that in more detail in the next chapter.

For now, the important thing to remember is that **an agent in CrewAI is not just a model. It is a role-bound, goal-driven component of an intelligent system.**

You shape its behavior by how you define it. The better you articulate its purpose and context, the more consistent and useful it becomes.

To internalize this, try an exercise: define two agents that perform the same task, but with completely different roles and goals.

For instance:

A "Marketing Strategist" whose goal is to write persuasive content.

A "Compliance Officer" whose goal is to ensure legal and ethical accuracy.

Then assign both the same task:

"Write a summary of our new AI feature for the product launch announcement."

What you'll find is that the outputs will be meaningfully different—not because the task changed, but because the agent's perspective shaped the response.

That's the core of agent-based system design: controlling not just what is done, but *how* it's done.

Agent Roles, Goals, and Capabilities

When you're building agent systems with CrewAI, one of the most important decisions you'll make is how you define the **roles** and **goals** of your agents.

These are not just labels—they are behavioral design instructions. They shape how each agent interprets its task, what tone it uses, what tools it activates, and how it responds to ambiguity.

If you define your agents with clarity, they'll consistently act in line with their purpose. If you define them vaguely—or skip defining a goal altogether—you'll find that their behavior becomes unpredictable, or even useless for complex workflows. So it's worth taking this seriously, even when your agents are just interacting with simple prompts.

Let's begin by exploring the meaning of "role" in CrewAI.

When you define an agent's role, you're telling the underlying language model *who it is supposed to be* during execution. This acts as a behavioral anchor. A role could be a job title, a domain identity, or a persona that guides the tone, depth, and focus of that agent's reasoning.

Here's an example:

```python
from crewai import Agent
from langchain.chat_models import ChatOpenAI

llm = ChatOpenAI(model_name="gpt-4",
temperature=0.3)

risk_analyst = Agent(
    role="Risk Assessment Specialist",
    goal="Evaluate business decisions and identify
associated risks before action is taken",
    backstory="You work as a strategic advisor to
business leaders, helping them assess potential
liabilities in financial, legal, and operational
domains.",
    llm=llm,
    verbose=True
)
```

Now every time this agent receives a task, it is not just answering from the perspective of a generic chatbot. It's responding as a **risk analyst** with a specific intention: to evaluate and flag risks.

55

If you gave the same task to a different agent—say, one with the role of "Growth Marketing Strategist"—the answer would reflect a completely different mindset. That's the strength of clearly defining a role. It gives the LLM a reason to behave in a certain way.

The **goal** is equally important. While the role defines identity, the goal defines purpose. It tells the agent what it's meant to accomplish, even across different tasks. In CrewAI, the goal becomes a permanent part of the agent's prompt structure. This means every task the agent takes on is viewed through the lens of that goal.

Let me show you why this matters with a live example. Below, both agents are given the same task: "Summarize the impact of the new AI regulation announced this week."

The first agent is defined as follows:

```
policy_writer = Agent(
    role="Public Policy Analyst",
    goal="Explain regulatory policies to non-
experts and evaluate their impact on industry
stakeholders",
    backstory="You help translate complex
regulations into actionable insights for business
leaders and policymakers.",
    llm=llm
)
```

The second agent is:

```
compliance_auditor = Agent(
    role="Regulatory Compliance Auditor",
    goal="Ensure internal systems and operations
align with the latest regulatory standards and
legal obligations",
    backstory="You are responsible for identifying
compliance gaps and enforcing company adherence to
legal frameworks.",
    llm=llm
)
```

Same task. Two different agents. What happens?

The **policy analyst** will probably focus on how the new regulation will affect innovation, small businesses, and policy enforcement timelines. The **compliance auditor**, in contrast, will focus on specific reporting obligations, risk of non-compliance, and the operational impact on company workflows.

This is how CrewAI lets you design intelligent behavior with minimal code. You're not building decision trees or writing logic branches. You're shaping agent behavior by defining context, role, and goal—all of which are passed into the LLM's prompt engine behind the scenes.

Now let's add another layer: **capabilities**.

By default, an agent's capabilities are limited to language reasoning. But you can extend what an agent can *do* by giving it access to **tools**—custom functions or third-party APIs. A capability could be a web search tool, a Python calculator, a database query wrapper, or a custom script you expose to LangChain.

Here's a practical example that ties this all together.

You want to create an **AI Investment Research Assistant** who can analyze public companies and generate investment briefs. You'll define a role, a goal, and equip it with a search tool.

```
from langchain.tools import DuckDuckGoSearchRun

search = DuckDuckGoSearchRun()

investment_analyst = Agent(
    role="AI Investment Research Analyst",
    goal="Find, summarize, and report on AI
companies making strategic moves or launching new
products",
    backstory="You track the AI industry for
investors and produce digestible summaries with key
business insights.",
    tools=[search],
    llm=llm,
    verbose=True
)
```

Now if you assign this agent a task like:

"Find the three most recent AI startup acquisitions made by major cloud providers and summarize their strategic impact."

You'll get a much more actionable and focused response than if you passed the same request to a general-purpose assistant.

The capability to perform web search is what allows this agent to complete its goal successfully. Without it, it might hallucinate information or give outdated summaries. So tools are not optional in serious workflows. They are how agents interface with real-world data and act beyond the context window.

When you're designing agents in CrewAI, take a moment to write down the following before you even touch code:

Who is this agent representing? (role)

What is this agent always trying to achieve? (goal)

What knowledge or tone does it need to carry? (backstory)

What actions does it need to take or tools does it need to use? (capabilities)

Answering those questions will lead to agents that perform reliably, adapt well to different tasks, and behave like intelligent collaborators—not just generic LLM interfaces.

To apply this practically, try the following exercise:

Write a task that says:

"Summarize the risks and opportunities of adopting AI in supply chain optimization."

Then define two agents:

One with the role of "AI Strategy Consultant" and a goal focused on identifying business opportunities.

Another with the role of "Logistics Risk Officer" and a goal focused on identifying potential pitfalls in supply chain changes.

Run the same task with both agents using CrewAI, and compare their responses. You'll quickly see how role and goal definitions don't just shape the *output*, they shape the *thought process* that leads to that output.

Memory and Context Awareness

By default, CrewAI agents do not retain any memory between executions. Every time you run a crew, the agents begin with a clean slate. That might sound like a limitation, but it's actually a deliberate design choice. It gives you full control over what context is passed to an agent, and it avoids the confusion of having stale data or unintended context bleed into a new task.

But there are real scenarios where memory is not just helpful—it's necessary.

Let's say you're building a multi-agent assistant that helps users plan events, manage projects, or engage in an advisory session across multiple prompts or tasks. In those cases, agents need to maintain awareness of prior interactions so they can reason in context. Without memory, agents will repeat themselves, forget important decisions, and act as if every input is brand new.

So how do you give a CrewAI agent memory?

You do that by assigning it a memory module compatible with **LangChain**, the framework CrewAI is built on top of. LangChain offers multiple memory classes, such as `ConversationBufferMemory`, `SummaryBufferMemory`, and `VectorStoreRetrieverMemory`, each suited to different styles of context management.

Let's walk through how you can enable basic memory for an agent using `ConversationBufferMemory`. This class simply stores the conversation history as a growing buffer, and injects it back into the prompt during each new call.

Start by installing the LangChain memory dependency if you haven't already:

pip install langchain

Now you can set up a memory-enabled agent like this:

```
from crewai import Agent
from langchain.chat_models import ChatOpenAI
```

```python
from langchain.memory import
ConversationBufferMemory

llm = ChatOpenAI(model_name="gpt-4",
temperature=0.2)

memory = ConversationBufferMemory(
    memory_key="chat_history",
    return_messages=True
)

planner_agent = Agent(
    role="Event Planning Assistant",
    goal="Help the user organize an upcoming event
and keep track of their preferences across the
planning session",
    backstory="You are an experienced assistant
with a great memory for details. You keep track of
dates, preferences, and decisions throughout the
conversation.",
    llm=llm,
    memory=memory,
    verbose=True
)
```

In this example, `ConversationBufferMemory` is attached to the agent using the `memory` argument. Each time this agent processes a task, it will retain the previous messages it has seen and generated, and that chat history will be included in the next prompt.

Let's assign this agent two sequential tasks and see how memory helps it build context.

```python
from crewai import Task, Crew

task1 = Task(
    description="The user wants to plan a company
offsite. Start by asking where they would like to
host it and what dates they have in mind.",
    expected_output="A message that asks the user
for location and date preferences.",
    agent=planner_agent
```

```
)

task2 = Task(
    description="Based on the user's answer,
suggest three possible venues in that location that
match the event type and group size.",
    expected_output="A short list of venue
recommendations with descriptions.",
    agent=planner_agent,
    context=[task1]
)

crew = Crew(
    agents=[planner_agent],
    tasks=[task1, task2],
    verbose=True
)

result = crew.run()
print(result)
```

When you run this, the agent will retain the output of `task1` and use it to inform `task2`. That means the venue suggestions will be grounded in the location and date provided by the user—without you needing to manually pass that data around. This is an early but important step toward building intelligent, persistent, stateful agents.

Now let's look at another example where this matters even more.

Suppose you're building a **multi-turn product advisor**. The user is comparing different AI tools, and they want to ask follow-up questions. If the agent forgets what tool was discussed in the previous turn, the conversation becomes useless.

Here's how you might define an agent for that:

```
from langchain.memory import
ConversationBufferMemory

advisor_memory = ConversationBufferMemory(
    memory_key="chat_history",
    return_messages=True
```

```
)

product_advisor = Agent(
    role="AI Product Consultant",
    goal="Help users evaluate and compare AI
platforms based on their use case and priorities",
    backstory="You are an impartial, knowledgeable
consultant who has evaluated dozens of AI solutions
and helps users make informed decisions.",
    llm=llm,
    memory=advisor_memory,
    verbose=True
)
```

In a multi-step session, you could assign each user question as a new task, and the agent would maintain memory across those turns.

There are cases where a conversation buffer isn't enough—especially when your task history is long, or you need to summarize context to stay within model token limits. In those cases, you can use SummaryBufferMemory, which stores long-term history but generates a running summary instead of full chat logs.

Here's how to configure that:

```
from langchain.memory import
ConversationSummaryBufferMemory

summary_memory = ConversationSummaryBufferMemory(
    llm=llm,
    memory_key="summary"
)

summarizing_agent = Agent(
    role="Project Advisor",
    goal="Track decisions and summarize discussions
to help project teams stay aligned",
    backstory="You participate in planning sessions
and provide ongoing summaries to help teams stay on
the same page.",
    llm=llm,
    memory=summary_memory,
```

```
    verbose=True
)
```

Now the agent doesn't just store every message—it summarizes the conversation, which allows you to extend the interaction beyond token limits while still retaining key context.

When memory is involved, you should always test how your agent behaves over time. Log the prompts that are being constructed. Review whether the memory is improving the response quality, or if it's introducing noise. Sometimes memory causes agents to repeat information or make outdated assumptions, especially if the conversation shifts and older context becomes irrelevant.

You can also write your own custom memory logic if needed. For example, you could log the output of each task to a SQLite database or use a Redis store to persist context across user sessions. LangChain makes this extensible, and CrewAI is designed to pass those memory objects seamlessly into your agents.

Now, one important note about CrewAI's default `context` system: even if you don't use formal memory, you can still simulate basic memory between tasks using the `context` parameter in the `Task` constructor.

```
task2 = Task(
    description="Use the user's preferred location
and dates to recommend venues.",
    expected_output="List of suitable venues.",
    agent=planner_agent,
    context=[task1]  # Explicitly pass prior task
output
)
```

This context is static, not dynamic—but it works well for linear workflows where task order and data flow are predictable. Formal memory, on the other hand, allows your agents to evolve over time without needing that structure hardcoded in.

In short, memory allows your agents to feel more intelligent, more grounded, and more helpful—especially in long conversations or multi-task pipelines. But with that power comes the need to manage it carefully.

Use memory when you need continuity. Use explicit context when you need predictability. And always monitor how your agents behave as their awareness increases.

Managing Prompts and Behavioral Logic

When you're working with CrewAI, you're not writing raw prompts most of the time. Instead, you're defining agents with roles, goals, and tasks—and CrewAI takes care of building the prompt under the hood. But just because you're not writing prompts line by line doesn't mean prompt engineering disappears. It's just abstracted into the way you structure agents and tasks.

That abstraction is powerful, but only if you understand how to manage it. If your agent responds poorly—maybe the output is vague, off-topic, or repetitive—the issue almost always traces back to how its behavior is being shaped through the combination of its prompt context and logic structure.

Let's walk through how CrewAI builds behavioral logic, and how you can manage that to ensure consistent, accurate, and safe outputs.

Every time a task is assigned to an agent, CrewAI generates a structured prompt. This prompt is built using several inputs:

The agent's `role`, `goal`, and `backstory`

The task's `description` and `expected_output`

Any contextual inputs, such as previous task results or memory entries

Optionally, tool usage instructions (if tools are assigned to the agent)

The final prompt is assembled and passed to the underlying LLM—typically GPT-4, GPT-3.5, Claude, or another LangChain-compatible model.

Let's take a concrete example. Here's the agent definition:

```
from crewai import Agent
from langchain.chat_models import ChatOpenAI

llm = ChatOpenAI(model_name="gpt-4",
temperature=0.2)

editor = Agent(
```

```
    role="Content Editor",
    goal="Improve clarity, tone, and accuracy of
written technical content",
    backstory="You are a detail-oriented technical
editor who works on high-quality documentation and
blog posts for software engineers.",
    llm=llm,
    verbose=True
)
```

Now pair it with a task like this:

```
from crewai import Task

edit_task = Task(
    description="You've been given a first draft of
a blog post about serverless computing. Review it
and return an improved version with better
structure, clear examples, and corrected technical
terminology.",
    expected_output="A polished version of the blog
post that maintains original meaning but improves
structure and clarity.",
    agent=editor
)
```

The prompt sent to the LLM might look something like this (CrewAI builds it internally, but here's what it's conceptually generating):

You are a Content Editor.

Your goal is to improve clarity, tone, and accuracy of written technical content.

You are a detail-oriented technical editor who works on high-quality documentation and blog posts for software engineers.

Task: You've been given a first draft of a blog post about serverless computing. Review it and return an improved version with better structure, clear examples, and corrected technical terminology.

```
Expected Output: A polished version of the blog post that
maintains original meaning but improves structure and clarity.
```

```
[context here if provided]
```

```
Please perform the task now.
```

This is where behavioral logic lives. If the role, goal, or task wording is unclear, the model will behave inconsistently. If you're vague about what "improve" means, you'll get surface-level changes. If you're specific—like "split long paragraphs," or "replace passive voice with active voice"—you get more control.

One of the best ways to manage prompt quality in CrewAI is to be **precise in your task definitions**. Don't rely on the model to infer what you mean. Spell it out in the `expected_output` section. For example, if you want structured JSON, say so. If you want three paragraphs and no more, state it directly.

Here's an example that's too vague:

```
expected_output="A summary of the document."
```

Here's a better version:

```
expected_output="A three-paragraph summary that
includes: (1) the main argument, (2) key supporting
data, and (3) the conclusion. The summary should be
written in a neutral tone and avoid subjective
language."
```

The second version acts as a contract. You're telling the LLM what the shape of the output should be. That results in far fewer hallucinations, far fewer formatting issues, and more predictable downstream behavior—especially when this output becomes the input for another agent.

You can also embed simple logic into the goal or backstory if the agent must always act a certain way. For example:

```
goal="Ensure the user receives accurate financial
recommendations without offering investment advice."
```

This will guide the model to avoid legal or compliance issues—even if the task doesn't explicitly mention that constraint.

Now, what if you really do want to inject a fully custom prompt? You can override the structured behavior entirely by creating a wrapper agent or using LangChain's prompt templates. But that's usually unnecessary. Instead, modify the structure of description and expected_output to shape the behavior within CrewAI's default flow.

Let's take this one step further. Suppose your task requires a multi-part answer, and you want the agent to reason through it step by step. You can use few-shot prompt engineering inside the task itself.

```
description=(
    "You're given a customer support transcript.
Perform the following steps:\n"
    "1. Identify the customer's problem.\n"
    "2. Determine whether it was resolved.\n"
    "3. Suggest how this interaction could be
improved.\n"
    "\nExample:\n"
    "Transcript: 'Hi, I can't reset my password.
The link doesn't work.'\n"
    "Response: 'The problem is a broken password
reset link. It was not resolved. Suggest enabling
fallback 2FA recovery.'\n"
    "\nNow evaluate the following transcript:"
)
```

By including a structured example and numbered steps, you're essentially overriding how the model thinks through the task—even though the outer structure is still handled by CrewAI. This technique allows you to fine-tune logic without needing to write a separate prompt engine.

A few final notes on behavior control:

Use low temperature (0.0-0.3) for tasks that require consistency and determinism—such as formatting, classification, or code generation.

Use higher temperature (0.6-0.9) for tasks that benefit from creativity—such as naming, ideation, or copywriting.

Always run your agents in verbose mode during development so you can observe what prompt was constructed and how the LLM responded. This is critical for debugging misbehavior.

If you plan to let users interact directly with your agents, add guardrails in the form of static prompt phrases in the goal or task description. These are not enforced constraints, but with a well-configured model like GPT-4, they usually work.

To see how prompt structure can fail, try removing the `expected_output` from one of your tasks and watching what the agent does. You'll likely get wandering, unfocused responses—because the model has no frame for what "done" looks like.

When you manage behavioral logic correctly, agents stop acting like black boxes. They start behaving like professionals with job descriptions and expectations.

Best Practices for Designing Reusable Agents

If you're planning to build more than one CrewAI workflow—or if you're thinking about long-term maintainability—you should be designing your agents to be reusable. Reusability means your agents don't live inside a single script. It means they're modular, testable, and can be plugged into different crews, workflows, or environments without rewriting them each time.

Agents in CrewAI are Python objects. That gives you a lot of flexibility—but without some structure, it's easy to end up with tightly coupled definitions that are hard to debug, modify, or extend.

Let's go through how to properly design agents so that they can be reused across different tasks, projects, or domains without friction.

Start by defining each agent in its own dedicated Python file. That might sound trivial, but it makes a huge difference once your project grows. For example, let's say you're building a research pipeline and you have an agent responsible for industry research. Instead of declaring that agent inside your `main.py` script, create a new file called `agents/researcher.py`.

Inside that file, define a function that returns a configured agent:

```python
# agents/researcher.py

from crewai import Agent
from langchain.chat_models import ChatOpenAI
from langchain.tools import DuckDuckGoSearchRun

def get_researcher_agent():
    llm = ChatOpenAI(model_name="gpt-4",
temperature=0.3)
    search = DuckDuckGoSearchRun()

    return Agent(
        role="Technology Researcher",
        goal="Stay current with technology trends
and summarize findings for decision-makers",
        backstory="You specialize in analyzing
emerging technologies and identifying patterns in
industry developments.",
        tools=[search],
        llm=llm,
        verbose=True
    )
```

This function is now a reusable factory for your agent. You can import and use this agent in multiple crews, or even in a completely different project, without touching the internals of how it's built.

If you want to make this more flexible, you can parameterize the function:

```python
def get_researcher_agent(model_name="gpt-4",
temperature=0.3, tools=None):
    llm = ChatOpenAI(model_name=model_name,
temperature=temperature)
    tools = tools or [DuckDuckGoSearchRun()]

    return Agent(
        role="Technology Researcher",
        goal="Stay current with technology trends
and summarize findings for decision-makers",
        backstory="You specialize in analyzing
emerging technologies and identifying patterns in
industry developments.",
        tools=tools,
```

```
        llm=llm,
        verbose=True
    )
```

Now you can override the model or tools at runtime if needed, without duplicating code.

Reusable agents should be **stateless** by default unless your workflow requires persistent memory. That makes them easier to swap in and out, especially in crews where one agent might need to be replaced by another with similar responsibilities. If you do want agents with memory, pass the memory in explicitly from outside the agent definition. Don't hardcode it.

Here's how you might do that in a clean, reusable way:

```
from langchain.memory import
ConversationBufferMemory

def get_support_agent(memory=None):
    llm = ChatOpenAI(model_name="gpt-3.5-turbo",
temperature=0.2)

    return Agent(
        role="Customer Success Agent",
        goal="Help users troubleshoot product
issues and improve their experience",
        backstory="You are polite, empathetic, and
focused on solving problems efficiently.",
        llm=llm,
        memory=memory,
        verbose=True
    )
```

Then, in your workflow script:

```
from langchain.memory import
ConversationBufferMemory
from agents.support import get_support_agent

memory =
ConversationBufferMemory(return_messages=True)
support_agent = get_support_agent(memory=memory)
```

This keeps the agent clean and flexible, while still supporting memory when you need it.

Another best practice is to **separate agent logic from business logic**. Don't build domain-specific decision-making into the agent itself. Let the agent interpret and complete tasks. Let tasks carry the logic of *what* should be done. For example, if you're checking whether a document is compliant with a standard, the agent should be defined with a goal like:

"Evaluate whether documents follow required compliance guidelines and summarize any violations."

Then the specific regulation or standard—like GDPR, HIPAA, or ISO 27001—should be passed in through the task description, not baked into the agent.

That way, you can reuse the same compliance agent for different standards just by adjusting the task:

```
Task(
    description="Check this document for compliance
with GDPR article 5. Identify any data retention
violations.",
    expected_output="A list of any violations
found, each with a reference to the relevant GDPR
article.",
    agent=compliance_agent
)
```

This makes the agent reusable across multiple contexts without code changes.

You should also document your agents. This could be a short comment at the top of each agent file, or a simple manifest of what roles you've created. When your project reaches 10 or more agents, it's easy to lose track of what each one is responsible for. Here's an example of what that might look like at the top of a file:

```
"""
Agent: Technology Researcher
Role: Tracks AI, cloud, and data engineering
trends.
```

```
Goal: Provide accurate summaries of emerging
technologies and their business impact.
Tools: DuckDuckGo web search.
Typical Use: Paired with a technical writer to
generate research-backed blog posts or reports.
"""
```

This kind of internal documentation saves you and your team time down the road, especially when debugging workflows or onboarding contributors.

Also consider keeping your agents **testable**. Because an agent is just a Python object, you can easily write unit tests to confirm its definition hasn't changed unexpectedly. For example:

```
def test_researcher_agent_role():
    agent = get_researcher_agent()
    assert agent.role == "Technology Researcher"
```

This won't catch logic issues in the LLM's output, but it ensures your configurations stay stable as your project evolves.

Finally, when working in large teams or modular projects, it's smart to create a **central agent registry**. This could be a Python module like `agents/__init__.py` where all your agents are defined and exposed through standardized import paths. That gives your crews a consistent way to pull in agents without needing to know which file they came from.

To summarize: reusable agents are defined in their own files, configured via parameterized functions, decoupled from hardcoded logic, equipped with optional tools and memory, and documented in a way that anyone else on your team can understand and use them.

When you design agents this way, your CrewAI project scales naturally. You won't be rewriting agent code every time you need a new workflow. You'll be composing intelligent systems from modular, well-formed parts—just like you would with clean APIs or service objects in a backend application.

Chapter 4: Tasks and Tools

In CrewAI, agents are the "who," but tasks are the "what." Tasks give agents their instructions, their scope of responsibility, and—most importantly—the structure to act intelligently rather than improvisationally. Once you've built solid agents, your next step is learning how to craft tasks that are actionable, goal-aligned, and context-aware. Just as importantly, you'll learn how to give agents the tools they need to act on real-world data, APIs, or internal services.

This chapter is all about understanding that the combination of a well-defined agent, a clear task, and the right tools is what allows your CrewAI systems to move from impressive outputs to production-grade workflows.

Designing Structured, Actionable Tasks

Agents in CrewAI need direction. A well-designed agent knows *how* to think, but it doesn't know *what* to do until you give it a task. That's where the `Task` object comes in. A task tells the agent what you expect it to accomplish. It's the operational unit of work, and without it, an agent does nothing.

If the agent is the actor, the task is the script.

But not just any instruction will do. A good CrewAI task must be **structured**, **clear**, and **outcome-driven**. When you write tasks that are too vague, you force the agent to make decisions you should have made for it—about scope, format, and objective. This leads to inconsistent, untestable results. When you write tasks precisely, your agents become far more reliable, which is essential when building multi-step workflows or agent chains.

Let's go straight into a practical example.

Here's a basic task that might work—but leaves a lot of open questions:

```
from crewai import Task

task = Task(
    description="Summarize the latest trends in
AI.",
    expected_output="A short summary.",
    agent=some_agent
)
```

This might technically run, but what exactly is "latest"? What does "summary" mean? One paragraph? Five bullet points? Is it informal or professional? This kind of ambiguity invites guesswork from the model and weakens the entire workflow—especially if other tasks depend on this output.

Let's refine it into something structured and actionable:

```
task = Task(
    description=(
        "Identify the top three emerging trends in
artificial intelligence in the past 30 days. "
        "Focus on developments in model
architecture, regulatory changes, and real-world
deployments. "
        "Summarize each trend in a clear, technical
paragraph."
    ),
    expected_output=(
        "Three paragraphs, each describing one
trend. Include a credible source link for each, and
write in a factual, analytical tone."
    ),
    agent=some_agent
)
```

Now the agent knows exactly what kind of input it's working with, how many items to include, what style to use, how to structure the output, and what information must be present. This makes the task **deterministic**—not in the sense of producing exactly the same output every time, but in the sense of producing the *right kind* of output every time.

Passing Context Between Tasks

Structured tasks don't operate in isolation. In many workflows, one task feeds into the next. That's where CrewAI's context parameter comes in. You can pass the output of one or more tasks as context for a new task. This allows agents to build on each other's work—something that's critical in long-form content generation, data analysis pipelines, and multi-role automation scenarios.

Here's a working example.

Let's say you have two agents: a **researcher** and a **writer**. The first task gathers the input, and the second task transforms it into publishable content.

```python
from crewai import Task

research_task = Task(
    description=(
        "Use web search to gather the three most
impactful AI product launches in the past month. "
        "For each, describe the product, the
company behind it, and the impact it's expected to
have on the market."
    ),
    expected_output=(
        "A list of three products, each with a
short description, company name, and one-sentence
impact analysis."
    ),
    agent=researcher_agent
)

write_task = Task(
    description=(
        "Write a 600-word blog post titled 'This
Month in AI Innovation'. "
        "Use the research findings provided and
organize the post with an introduction, three body
sections (one for each product), and a conclusion."
    ),
    expected_output=(
        "Markdown-formatted blog post with clear
section headers and links to sources where
appropriate."
    ),
    agent=writer_agent,
    context=[research_task]
)
```

With this structure, the writer agent receives not just the task, but also the completed output of the research task—so it has the input it needs to operate intelligently. You don't need to write glue code to stitch together strings or inject prompt fragments. CrewAI handles that behind the scenes.

This enables clean, readable, and testable multi-step workflows.

Common Pitfalls When Writing Tasks

One of the most common mistakes is failing to specify **format** in the `expected_output`. This becomes a major issue when task outputs are being passed to downstream agents, APIs, or post-processing scripts. Always state clearly whether the output should be plain text, bullet points, JSON, Markdown, or some other structure.

Here's a weak `expected_output` definition:

```
expected_output="Summarized analysis of the document."
```

And here's a stronger, actionable one:

```
expected_output=(
    "A JSON object with three keys: 'summary',
'strengths', and 'weaknesses'. "
    "Each value should be a string no longer than
200 words."
)
```

When you do this, you're helping the model align its reasoning with your system's needs. You're also preparing the output to be passed to another task or consumed by a downstream tool or API.

Another common mistake is assigning a task that's too broad for a single agent to handle in one step. Tasks like "analyze this dataset and write a research report" are not actionable unless you break them down into smaller steps.

Split it instead:

Task 1: "Perform statistical analysis on the dataset and summarize key patterns."

Task 2: "Using the findings from the statistical analysis, draft a report with structured sections."

These can be assigned to different agents with different specialties—perhaps one focused on data analysis and another on technical writing.

Building Task Generators Dynamically

You might find yourself in a situation where tasks need to be generated based on user input or external data. In those cases, you can define Python functions that return tasks dynamically.

Here's how you could build a review task for any given product name:

```python
def create_review_task(product_name: str):
    return Task(
        description=f"Write a detailed, balanced product review for '{product_name}'. Include key features, pros and cons, and ideal use cases.",
        expected_output="Three paragraphs: Introduction, Review Body, and Conclusion. Write in an objective and helpful tone.",
        agent=review_agent
    )
```

This becomes especially useful when looping through user-provided data, or automating task generation in a dynamic workflow where the number or nature of tasks isn't known in advance.

You can also construct tasks with template data from a database or external system. This gives you full flexibility in building workflows that are data-driven and scalable.

Tasks in CrewAI are not just prompts –they are structured interfaces between your agents and your goals. Writing good tasks means thinking clearly about what you want from the agent, how you'll use the output, and how the task fits into the larger system.

If you treat tasks as first-class objects—just like you would treat classes or functions in a well-structured application—you'll build workflows that are robust, maintainable, and scalable.

Dynamic Prompt Templates

In most cases, you won't be building static, hard-coded agents or tasks. You'll be working in live applications, batch automation pipelines, or user-facing tools where the input to each task varies depending on real-time data. That's where **dynamic prompt templates** come in.

CrewAI allows you to build tasks and workflows programmatically—generating prompt content on the fly using Python string formatting. This lets you insert user data, API results, database records, or file content into your tasks in a clean, maintainable way.

The key principle here is this: **you don't need to manually write a new task every time the input changes. You generate the task dynamically.**

Let's walk through a simple example to show this in action.

Suppose you're building a product review assistant. Each time a new product is submitted to your system, you want to create a task for your agent to write a review. The only thing that changes is the product name and category.

Here's how you would define a reusable function that takes those inputs and generates a `Task` object on demand:

```python
from crewai import Task

def create_review_task(product_name: str, category:
str, agent):
    return Task(
        description=(
            f"Write a structured, professional
review of the product '{product_name}', "
            f"which falls under the category
'{category}'. Focus on usability, features, and
potential limitations. "
            "Make sure to keep the tone balanced
and factual."
        ),
        expected_output=(
            "Three sections: Introduction, Key
Features and Performance, and Conclusion. "
            "Each section should be around 100
words. Use Markdown formatting."
        ),
        agent=agent
    )
```

Now, instead of defining a different task for every product, you can generate tasks dynamically as you loop through data:

```python
products = [
    {"name": "StreamlineAI", "category": "Workflow
Automation"},
    {"name": "CodeGuard", "category": "Developer
Tools"},
    {"name": "EcoLens", "category": "Environmental
Monitoring"},
]

for product in products:
    task = create_review_task(product["name"],
product["category"], review_agent)
    crew = Crew(agents=[review_agent],
tasks=[task])
    result = crew.run()
    print(f"\nReview for
{product['name']}:\n{result}")
```

This is more than just a convenience—it's a foundational design pattern for scalable agent systems. Whether you're processing form input, Slack messages, spreadsheet rows, or emails, this pattern allows you to dynamically create context-aware task instructions without sacrificing clarity or structure.

You can use this exact same approach to handle personalized messages, marketing copy, documentation updates, or automated test generation.

Let's try a more advanced example.

You're building an internal assistant that receives a support request from a ticketing system and creates a task for your support agent to reply to the customer.

Here's how you might model that:

```python
def create_support_response_task(ticket_id: str,
issue_summary: str, customer_name: str, agent):
    return Task(
        description=(
            f"You are handling a customer support
request submitted under Ticket ID: {ticket_id}. "
            f"The customer, {customer_name},
reports the following
issue:\n\n'{issue_summary}'\n\n"
```

```
            "Craft a helpful and empathetic reply
that either solves the issue or provides a clear
next step."
            ),
        expected_output=(
            "An email-style response written in a
professional tone. Include a greeting and sign-off.
"
            "Keep the message under 200 words
unless additional detail is required."
            ),
        agent=agent
    )
```

Here's what calling that might look like in your automation logic:

```
ticket = {
    "id": "REQ-4821",
    "issue": "I keep getting a 403 error when
trying to download my report from the dashboard.",
    "customer": "Marisol"
}

support_task = create_support_response_task(
    ticket_id=ticket["id"],
    issue_summary=ticket["issue"],
    customer_name=ticket["customer"],
    agent=support_agent
)

crew = Crew(agents=[support_agent],
tasks=[support_task])
print(crew.run())
```

The agent now has *specific*, personalized input tied to a real user problem. And because the rest of your structure is consistent, you don't need to hand-tune anything. You get reusable logic with variable content.

This technique also becomes essential when your tasks depend on data pulled from external services. Say you're generating summaries of stock performance based on API data. You can extract what you need, format it into a task, and hand it to a financial analyst agent.

Here's an example using fictional API data:

```python
def create_stock_summary_task(symbol: str,
company_name: str, recent_data: dict, agent):
    return Task(
        description=(
            f"Create a one-paragraph summary of
recent stock performance for {company_name}
({symbol}). "
            f"The latest metrics are: Open:
{recent_data['open']}, Close:
{recent_data['close']}, "
            f"Volume: {recent_data['volume']}, and
5-day trend: {recent_data['trend']}."
        ),
        expected_output=(
            "A paragraph with observations on
volatility, recent trends, and whether the stock is
gaining or losing momentum. "
            "Avoid giving financial advice."
        ),
        agent=agent
    )
```

There's no need to modify the agent or rebuild the task logic—just pass in the dynamic content. Your tasks are now templates with data injected at runtime, producing highly relevant and reliable instructions for the agent to execute.

You can take this even further by building task queues that ingest incoming data, construct tasks dynamically, and execute them automatically. CrewAI supports that pattern without any special configuration because tasks are just Python objects. That gives you full control using native language constructs.

The key is to **be explicit about what changes and what stays fixed**. You want your templates to be predictable in their structure, even when the values they contain are dynamic. Don't just paste user input raw into a prompt—wrap it with context and constraints so the agent knows how to interpret it.

For example, instead of this:

description=f"Analyze this feedback: {feedback}"

Do this:

```
description=(
    f"The following customer feedback was
received:\n\n'{feedback}'\n\n"
    "Identify whether the tone is positive,
neutral, or negative, and extract the main issue
mentioned. "
    "Provide your answer in two short bullet
points."
)
```

The structure of your prompt should never be ambiguous just because the data is dynamic.

To reinforce this, try writing a task template that generates a changelog based on a list of recent commits. Pass the list in as a formatted string, and ask your agent to turn that into user-facing release notes.

```
def create_changelog_task(commits: list[str],
agent):
    commit_block = "\n".join(f"- {commit}" for
commit in commits)

    return Task(
        description=(
            "You are creating user-facing release
notes based on the following commit messages:\n\n"
            f"{commit_block}\n\n"
            "Group similar changes together, and
write in a friendly, readable style."
        ),
        expected_output="A Markdown changelog with
sections for 'New Features', 'Improvements', and
'Fixes'.",
        agent=agent
    )
```

With this pattern, you can dynamically generate any number of tasks, for any kind of agent, from any structured input. And because your structure remains predictable, your workflows remain testable and reliable.

Integrating Tools: APIs, Web Access, DBs

Agents powered by language models are strong reasoning engines, but they're only as useful as the data and actions available to them. Without external tools, agents are limited to the knowledge inside the model's context window—and that means they can hallucinate, produce outdated information, or fall short when real-time data or actionable outputs are needed.

To address this, CrewAI allows agents to use tools: wrappers around real-world functions that enable access to APIs, live web data, local scripts, databases, or any custom Python logic you provide.

Once you give an agent access to a tool, it can choose to call that tool when completing a task. This transforms the agent from a passive responder into an interactive operator. Instead of relying entirely on its internal knowledge, it can now look up information, calculate results, or fetch documents on demand.

Let's start with a basic integration, and then move step by step into more advanced use cases.

Web Search as a Tool

LangChain provides a few built-in tools that are immediately useful. One of the simplest and most effective is DuckDuckGoSearchRun, which allows your agent to query the public internet for current data.

Start by installing the required dependency if you haven't already:

`pip install duckduckgo-search`

Then import and use it with CrewAI like this:

```
from langchain.tools import DuckDuckGoSearchRun
from crewai import Agent
from langchain.chat_models import ChatOpenAI

search_tool = DuckDuckGoSearchRun()
llm = ChatOpenAI(model_name="gpt-4",
temperature=0.3)

research_agent = Agent(
    role="Technology Trend Researcher",
```

```
    goal="Track emerging technologies and provide
briefings on recent innovations",
    backstory="You are a research analyst who uses
internet search to stay on top of the latest
developments.",
    tools=[search_tool],
    llm=llm,
    verbose=True
)
```

Once that tool is assigned, the agent will decide when to use it during task execution. You don't need to instruct it step by step. Instead, the tool is exposed in the background, and the model will determine if it's necessary based on the task.

Assign a task like this:

```
from crewai import Task

task = Task(
    description="Search for and summarize three
recent breakthroughs in robotics within the last
two weeks.",
    expected_output="A list of three items, each
with a short description and a source link.",
    agent=research_agent
)
```

When this task is executed, the agent will likely invoke the search tool behind the scenes to gather real-time data—because the model understands that its own training data may be outdated for that kind of request.

You don't need to manage tool execution yourself. The agent uses the LangChain tools plugin system to determine when and how to call the appropriate tool function based on natural language reasoning.

Calling External APIs

Web search is useful, but many business workflows need access to specific external APIs—such as a CRM, weather feed, financial market data, or your own internal services.

You can expose any API as a tool simply by writing a Python function that calls it, and wrapping that function in a LangChain `Tool` object. Let's go through an example step-by-step.

Say you want your agent to look up current weather for a city using the OpenWeatherMap API.

First, install `requests` if you don't already have it:

pip install requests

Now, write a wrapper function:

```
import requests

def get_weather(city: str):
    api_key = "your_openweathermap_api_key"
    url =
f"https://api.openweathermap.org/data/2.5/weather?q
={city}&appid={api_key}&units=metric"

    response = requests.get(url)
    if response.status_code != 200:
        return f"Failed to fetch weather data for
{city}."

    data = response.json()
    temp = data['main']['temp']
    description = data['weather'][0]['description']
    return f"The current temperature in {city} is
{temp}°C with {description}."
```

Now turn it into a LangChain-compatible tool:

```
from langchain.tools import Tool

weather_tool = Tool(
    name="Get Weather",
    func=get_weather,
    description="Provides current weather data for
a given city using OpenWeatherMap."
)
```

Assign it to an agent:

```
weather_agent = Agent(
    role="Weather Information Assistant",
    goal="Provide real-time weather updates to
users based on their location",
    backstory="You specialize in checking real-time
forecasts via trusted weather APIs.",
    tools=[weather_tool],
    llm=llm,
    verbose=True
)
```

Now this agent is capable of live API calls. When given a task like:

```
Task(
    description="Get the current weather in Paris
and describe what kind of clothing someone should
wear today.",
    expected_output="One short paragraph describing
temperature, conditions, and clothing advice.",
    agent=weather_agent
)
```

The agent will invoke the weather tool, receive the temperature and condition, and then complete the task using that data. All you had to do was make the API available as a callable function.

Querying Databases

You can do the same with SQL databases. Suppose you have an internal SQLite database of customer feedback, and you want an agent to pull a random feedback message.

Here's a basic example using `sqlite3`:

```
import sqlite3

def get_random_feedback():
    conn = sqlite3.connect("feedback.db")
    cursor = conn.cursor()

    cursor.execute("SELECT message FROM feedback
ORDER BY RANDOM() LIMIT 1")
    result = cursor.fetchone()
```

```
    conn.close()

    return result[0] if result else "No feedback
found."
```

Wrap it as a tool:

```
feedback_tool = Tool(
    name="Customer Feedback Lookup",
    func=get_random_feedback,
    description="Retrieves a random feedback
message from the customer database."
)
```

Assign it to a QA or analysis agent, and now your agent can retrieve database content and analyze it, summarize it, or pass it to another agent as part of a workflow.

There is no technical limit to what your tools can do—file access, cloud APIs, graph queries, machine learning models, you name it. As long as your function returns a string and can be called with one argument (or is wrapped to conform), you can turn it into a usable tool.

The only constraint is that LangChain tools expect synchronous execution. If you're calling async APIs, you'll need to manage them inside a synchronous wrapper or use thread-safe execution models.

Tools turn CrewAI agents from conversational models into active, capable systems. They are the bridge between what the agent *knows* and what it can *do*. Whether you're building an internal assistant, a data automation bot, or a production content generator, tool integration is what enables real-world value.

Creating Custom Tools with Python

Giving an agent the ability to use tools is what makes it interactive and capable—not just generative. CrewAI relies on LangChain under the hood, and LangChain treats tools as callable Python functions that the agent can use as part of its reasoning process. This means that anything you can write in Python—whether it's calling an API, querying a file, summarizing a document, or running a local script—can be exposed as a tool for an agent to use.

When you're building your own tool, the most important thing is to structure it in a way the agent can understand and reliably call. That means the function must be predictable, accept the right inputs, and return clean, readable output that the agent can work with.

Let's walk through this step by step.

Step 1: Define a Python Function That Does Something Useful

Start with a plain Python function. For this example, we'll build a tool that fetches the current exchange rate between two currencies using the ExchangeRate API. You can register and get a free API key.

Here's a basic implementation:

```python
import requests

def get_exchange_rate(query: str) -> str:
    """Expects input like 'USD to EUR'."""
    try:
        from_currency, to_currency =
query.upper().split(" to ")
    except ValueError:
        return "Please provide input in the format
'USD to EUR'."

    api_key = "your_api_key_here"
    url = f"https://v6.exchangerate-
api.com/v6/{api_key}/pair/{from_currency}/{to_curre
ncy}"

    response = requests.get(url)
    if response.status_code != 200:
        return "Failed to fetch exchange rate."

    data = response.json()
    rate = data.get("conversion_rate")
    if rate:
        return f"The exchange rate from
{from_currency} to {to_currency} is {rate}."
```

```
    return "Exchange rate not found."
```

This function expects input as a single string (which is how LangChain calls tools), and returns a formatted string.

Step 2: Wrap It as a LangChain Tool

Now you need to wrap this function using LangChain's `Tool` class so that CrewAI can expose it to the agent.

```
from langchain.tools import Tool

exchange_tool = Tool(
    name="Currency Exchange Rate",
    func=get_exchange_rate,
    description=(
        "Provides real-time exchange rate data
between two currencies. "
        "Input format: 'USD to EUR'. Returns the
current conversion rate."
    )
)
```

The `name` should be a short identifier. The `description` is what the language model reads in order to decide when and how to use the tool. This is very important—models rely entirely on that text to understand the purpose and format of the tool.

Step 3: Assign the Tool to an Agent

Now define an agent and assign the tool:

```
from crewai import Agent
from langchain.chat_models import ChatOpenAI

llm = ChatOpenAI(model_name="gpt-4",
temperature=0.3)

finance_agent = Agent(
    role="Financial Assistant",
    goal="Answer user questions about currency
values using up-to-date exchange rates.",
```

```
    backstory="You help users convert money and
understand currency values across markets.",
    tools=[exchange_tool],
    llm=llm,
    verbose=True
)
```

You can now give this agent a task like:

```
from crewai import Task

task = Task(
    description="What is the exchange rate from USD
to JPY?",
    expected_output="A sentence reporting the
current exchange rate from USD to JPY.",
    agent=finance_agent
)
```

When the task is run, the agent will reason about the request, recognize that it needs current data, and call the `Currency Exchange Rate` tool using the correct format.

Step 4: Build Tools That Accept and Format Structured Input

If your tool expects something more complex than a single string—like a JSON payload or a table—it's often best to keep the input simple and do the parsing inside the tool itself.

Here's an example tool that accepts a product name and fetches its description from a fake internal catalog (represented here as a Python dictionary):

```
def lookup_product(product_name: str) -> str:
    catalog = {
        "StreamlineAI": "A platform that automates
data workflows for enterprise teams.",
        "CodeGuard": "A static analysis tool that
flags risky code patterns in CI pipelines.",
        "EcoLens": "A dashboard for real-time
environmental sensor data from remote sites."
    }
```

```
    return catalog.get(product_name.strip(),
"Product not found.")
```

Wrap it as:

```
product_tool = Tool(
    name="Product Info Lookup",
    func=lookup_product,
    description="Returns a product description when
given the product name. Input should be a single
name like 'CodeGuard'."
)
```

Give this tool to a content writer agent:

```
product_agent = Agent(
    role="Product Content Specialist",
    goal="Write marketing blurbs and feature
summaries based on product information.",
    backstory="You work with technical product
managers to explain products to non-technical
customers.",
    tools=[product_tool],
    llm=llm,
    verbose=True
)
```

You can now create a task that invites the agent to use the tool to gather product descriptions before writing the content.

```
Task(
    description="Write a two-sentence product blurb
for EcoLens.",
    expected_output="Two sentences suitable for a
landing page hero section.",
    agent=product_agent
)
```

The agent will detect that it has access to a tool that can help, and query `lookup_product("EcoLens")` under the hood, integrating the result into the generated copy.

Step 5: Best Practices for Custom Tool Design

To ensure your tools are reliable and usable by agents:

Keep inputs simple—prefer one-argument functions. If needed, format multiple parameters as a single input string and parse it inside the function.

Make return values clean, concise, and ready to drop into a natural language response.

Use informative, instructional `description` fields. These directly influence how and when the model chooses to call the tool.

Avoid tools with side effects unless you're managing the consequences. If a tool sends emails, makes irreversible API calls, or triggers financial transactions, build in extra confirmation steps or guardrails.

Log tool usage during development. This helps you see when and how the model decides to invoke the tool, and what input it provides.

Here's a basic logging wrapper you can apply around any function:

```python
def log_tool_call(func):
    def wrapper(arg):
        print(f"[Tool Called] {func.__name__} with input: {arg}")
        return func(arg)
    return wrapper

lookup_product = log_tool_call(lookup_product)
```

This makes debugging significantly easier, especially when agents are executing tasks asynchronously or calling multiple tools.

By writing your own tools in Python, you unlock the full power of CrewAI. You're no longer limited to what the language model knows or guesses—you can hand it real capabilities, controlled through your own code. This allows you to build agents that work with your data, your APIs, and your processes with precision and repeatability.

Tool Chaining and Agent-Tool Interactions

At its core, CrewAI enables you to build systems where agents don't just generate language—they complete tasks by reasoning, using tools, and interacting with each other. One of the most powerful concepts that emerges from this is **tool chaining**—the ability for an agent to use a tool, act on the output, and either continue processing it or pass it forward to another agent or system.

Tool chaining happens when the output of one tool becomes the input to a second tool—or to another agent's task. This lets you build multi-stage workflows where decisions, calculations, lookups, and transformations happen in sequence, all within the context of an orchestrated crew.

Scenario: Automated Customer Feedback Report

You're building a system to process customer feedback from a database, analyze the sentiment, extract common themes, and generate a report for a product team. This involves three distinct operations:

Retrieve customer feedback from your database.

Use a sentiment analysis tool to classify each message.

Pass the processed results to a writer agent to generate a report.

Each of those steps can be handled by a tool or agent. The trick is managing the **intermediate data** between each step and keeping everything structured so the handoffs don't fall apart.

Step 1: Feedback Retrieval Tool

Let's start by building a tool that pulls five feedback messages from your database. We'll simulate it here with a hardcoded function for demonstration:

```python
def get_recent_feedback(dummy_input: str) -> str:
    feedback_entries = [
        "I love the product, but the onboarding was
confusing.",
        "Customer support was slow to respond.",
        "Great UX, very intuitive interface.",
        "The reporting dashboard crashes often.",
        "It's saving me 10 hours a week—worth every
dollar."
    ]
    return "\n".join(f"- {entry}" for entry in
feedback_entries)
```

Wrap this as a tool:

```
from langchain.tools import Tool

feedback_tool = Tool(
    name="Fetch Customer Feedback",
    func=get_recent_feedback,
    description="Returns a list of the five most
recent feedback messages."
)
```

Step 2: Sentiment Analysis Tool

Now build a sentiment analyzer. For now, let's simulate it with simple keyword matching. In production, you'd plug this into a local ML model or external API.

```
def analyze_sentiment(batch: str) -> str:
    lines = batch.strip().split("\n")
    output = []

    for line in lines:
        msg = line.strip("- ").lower()
        if "love" in msg or "great" in msg or
"saving" in msg:
            label = "Positive"
        elif "confusing" in msg or "slow" in msg or
"crashes" in msg:
            label = "Negative"
        else:
            label = "Neutral"
        output.append(f"{line} → Sentiment:
{label}")

    return "\n".join(output)
```

Wrap that as a tool:

```
sentiment_tool = Tool(
    name="Sentiment Analyzer",
    func=analyze_sentiment,
```

```
    description="Classifies each feedback entry as
Positive, Negative, or Neutral. Input should be a
list of feedback lines."

)
```

Step 3: Create a CrewAI Agent That Uses These Tools

Now you define an agent that has access to both tools and a task that asks the agent to perform both actions in one go. CrewAI doesn't require you to define tool sequences manually—the agent figures out what tools to use and when based on the task prompt and tool descriptions.

Here's the agent setup:

```
from crewai import Agent
from langchain.chat_models import ChatOpenAI

llm = ChatOpenAI(model_name="gpt-4",
temperature=0.2)

analysis_agent = Agent(
    role="Customer Feedback Analyst",
    goal="Review recent customer feedback, classify
sentiment, and prepare a summary for the product
team.",
    backstory="You are responsible for identifying
key trends in user feedback by using internal tools
and preparing weekly summaries.",
    tools=[feedback_tool, sentiment_tool],
    llm=llm,
    verbose=True
)
```

Here's the task:

```
from crewai import Task

feedback_task = Task(
    description=(
        "Fetch the most recent customer feedback
using the feedback tool. "
        "Then use the sentiment analysis tool to
classify each entry. "
```

```
        "Summarize how many entries fall under each
sentiment category, and provide two example quotes
per category."
    ),
    expected_output=(
        "A report with three sections: Positive,
Neutral, and Negative. Each section should include
a count and two quotes."
    ),
    agent=analysis_agent
)
```

Now run the crew:

```
from crewai import Crew

crew = Crew(agents=[analysis_agent],
tasks=[feedback_task], verbose=True)
result = crew.run()
print(result)
```

The agent will perform the full chain:

Call the feedback tool to get raw input.

Pass that input to the sentiment tool.

Parse the results, group them, extract quotes.

Format a structured report that satisfies the task.

This is tool chaining—driven by the agent's ability to reason, decide which tool to use, and operate across multiple steps with minimal orchestration on your part.

Controlling Tool Handoff Between Agents

In more advanced workflows, you may want different agents to specialize. One agent retrieves and processes data; another interprets and writes a report. You can accomplish this by splitting the task and passing results using the context field.

Agent A: uses tools to fetch and annotate data.
Agent B: receives Agent A's result and writes a user-friendly output.

```
data_task = Task(
    description="Fetch recent feedback and classify
sentiment using tools.",
    expected_output="A structured list with
sentiment labels and messages.",
    agent=analysis_agent
)

writer_agent = Agent(
    role="Customer Insights Writer",
    goal="Create a product insights memo based on
analyzed feedback.",
    backstory="You turn annotated feedback into
internal memos that influence roadmap decisions.",
    llm=llm,
    verbose=True
)

summary_task = Task(
    description="Write a summary of customer
sentiment trends using the analysis results.",
    expected_output="A three-paragraph executive
summary with clear recommendations.",
    agent=writer_agent,
    context=[data_task]
)
```

The result is a pipeline where each agent focuses on its specialty, and intermediate results are passed as structured text.

Tool Chaining Considerations

A few things to keep in mind when designing these workflows:

Tools must be deterministic and testable. If a tool fails, your chain breaks.

Output formatting matters. Downstream agents or tasks should be designed to expect consistent structure.

Agents don't remember what tool they used. The logic happens during each task run, based on reasoning.

You can simulate multi-step chains by embedding action plans inside the task description—e.g., "Step 1: Fetch. Step 2: Analyze. Step 3: Report."

This gives you all the flexibility of traditional procedural workflows, but with the flexibility and abstraction of agent reasoning.

Tool chaining is how you build full pipelines, not just one-off queries. It allows your agents to go beyond language into structured, multi-step decision making and action execution.

Chapter 5: Crews and Coordination

In the previous chapters, we've explored the foundational elements of CrewAI—agents, tasks, and tools. Now, let's focus on how these components come together to form a cohesive unit known as a **Crew**. This chapter will guide you through the intricacies of assembling and coordinating a Crew, ensuring that your AI agents collaborate effectively to accomplish complex tasks.

Defining and Assembling a Crew

When you've got your agents, tools, and tasks ready, you still need a mechanism to coordinate their interaction. In CrewAI, this coordination happens inside a structure called a **Crew**. A Crew is where everything comes together—it's where you define which agents are involved, what tasks they need to perform, how they should process them, and in what order those tasks should be completed.

In practical terms, a Crew is just a Python object that brings together agents and tasks under a defined process model. But conceptually, it's what lets multiple agents function as a single intelligent system rather than isolated workers.

The structure of a Crew is what enables task handoffs, structured communication, and consistent workflow execution.

Let's go step by step and walk through how to define and assemble a complete Crew using CrewAI.

Step 1: Create Your Agents

Each agent needs to be clearly defined with a role, goal, and backstory. This information sets the behavioral context for how the agent will interpret and complete tasks.

Here's an example of two agents: one responsible for technical research, and another for writing content based on that research.

```
from crewai import Agent
from langchain.chat_models import ChatOpenAI
```

```python
llm = ChatOpenAI(model_name="gpt-4",
temperature=0.2)

researcher = Agent(
    role="AI Industry Researcher",
    goal="Identify the most impactful AI trends and
synthesize them into digestible insights.",
    backstory="You are an expert in machine
learning and tech forecasting, working with cross-
functional teams to spot what matters.",
    llm=llm,
    verbose=True
)

writer = Agent(
    role="Content Strategist",
    goal="Write clear and engaging articles based
on technical research for a business audience.",
    backstory="You translate complex topics into
accessible narratives for executives and product
teams.",
    llm=llm,
    verbose=True
)
```

These agents aren't doing anything on their own yet, but once you assign tasks to them and assemble them into a Crew, they become active participants in a collaborative process.

Step 2: Define the Tasks

Each agent needs at least one task assigned. A task should tell the agent what it's supposed to accomplish, what the output should look like, and—optionally—what context it needs.

Let's create a task for the researcher and one for the writer.

```python
from crewai import Task

research_task = Task(
    description="Summarize three key developments
in artificial intelligence from the past 30 days.
```

```
Focus on model releases, regulatory updates, and
commercial deployments.",
    expected_output=(
        "Three clearly labeled sections, each
summarizing one development with a short paragraph
and a source link."
    ),
    agent=researcher
)

writing_task = Task(
    description="Based on the research findings,
write a 600-word article titled 'AI Trends to Watch
This Month'. Include an intro, three main sections,
and a closing paragraph.",
    expected_output="A complete Markdown-formatted
article ready for blog publishing.",
    agent=writer,
    context=[research_task]
)
```

The second task references the first one using the `context` parameter. This
tells the Crew that the writer agent must wait for the output of the research
task before starting its work.

Step 3: Assemble the Crew

Once your agents and tasks are defined, you can assemble them into a Crew.
This is where you decide how the tasks should be processed—sequentially, in
parallel, or under the direction of a manager agent.

Let's build a sequential crew, where tasks are executed in order:

```
from crewai import Crew, Process

crew = Crew(
    agents=[researcher, writer],
    tasks=[research_task, writing_task],
    process=Process.sequential,   # Ensures one task
completes before the next begins
    verbose=True
)
```

Calling `crew.run()` will execute the full workflow, triggering each agent in turn and passing context between them:

```
result = crew.run()
print(result)
```

If you enable `verbose=True`, you'll see logs of what each agent is doing, when tools are invoked, and how outputs are passed forward. This is especially helpful for debugging or optimizing workflows.

Step 4: Running a Real Use Case

Let's say you're part of a content operations team in a SaaS company, and each month, your marketing lead asks for a trends report. With a Crew like the one above, you can automate this process. You can even connect this crew to a scheduler or webhook so that it runs every 30 days, pulling live data, formatting it, and sending it to the CMS.

You could extend the system by adding another agent whose role is to fact-check the article or translate it into other languages—each assigned their own tasks and roles, all assembled into a larger Crew.

Here's how that might look with a third agent:

```
editor = Agent(
    role="Technical Editor",
    goal="Review technical articles for clarity,
accuracy, and logical flow.",
    backstory="You are a meticulous editor with
experience reviewing AI-related publications.",
    llm=llm,
    verbose=True
)

editing_task = Task(
    description="Review the blog article for
clarity, coherence, and technical accuracy. Provide
inline suggestions if necessary.",
    expected_output="The revised Markdown-formatted
article, edited and polished for publication.",
    agent=editor,
    context=[writing_task]
```

```
)

crew = Crew(
    agents=[researcher, writer, editor],
    tasks=[research_task, writing_task,
editing_task],
    process=Process.sequential,
    verbose=True
)
```

Now you have a fully structured, end-to-end content production pipeline that mimics what human teams do—but with AI agents following your rules and structure.

Defining and assembling a Crew is more than just linking components—it's how you construct workflows that are purposeful, accountable, and extensible. By giving agents focused responsibilities and defining tasks that reflect your business logic, you can build agent-based systems that deliver real outcomes—not just chatbot responses.

Sequential, Hierarchical, and Custom Process Handlers

Once you've defined a set of agents and tasks, the next step is deciding **how** those tasks should be coordinated and executed. This is where the **process handler** comes into play. In CrewAI, the process defines the execution strategy used to guide task flow and agent interaction. The right choice here directly affects the quality, speed, and clarity of your system's outputs.

CrewAI currently supports three main process modes:

`sequential`: tasks are completed one after another, in order

`hierarchical`: a manager agent oversees execution and decision-making

`custom`: you define your own execution logic to fit specialized workflows

Each approach serves a different purpose and fits different kinds of problems. Let's go through each one with examples, practical implementation, and key things to watch out for.

Sequential Process

The sequential handler is the simplest to understand and the most widely used. It ensures that tasks are executed one at a time, in the exact order they were defined. The output of one task becomes available to the next task (if referenced via context), allowing for step-by-step workflows that are predictable and easy to debug.

Let's say you have a workflow with three agents:

A **researcher** who gathers market trends

A **writer** who turns that into an article

An **editor** who checks it for polish

Each of their tasks builds on the previous one. Here's how you'd configure that:

```
from crewai import Crew, Process

crew = Crew(
    agents=[researcher, writer, editor],
    tasks=[research_task, writing_task,
editing_task],
    process=Process.sequential,
    verbose=True
)
```

When you call crew.run(), the researcher completes their task first. Once finished, the writer gets access to the research result as context and generates the article. Then the editor works on the article using the writer's output as their input.

This flow is reliable and deterministic, which makes it ideal when each task depends on accurate completion of the previous one. It also ensures that only one agent is working at any moment, so if you're working within API rate limits or cost constraints, it's more manageable.

Where it might fall short is in speed or flexibility—if tasks are independent and could run in parallel, sequential processing would unnecessarily slow things down.

Hierarchical Process

When a project requires oversight, decisions about task delegation, or real-time adjustment based on output quality, the `hierarchical` handler is more appropriate. This process introduces a **manager agent**—a special agent whose job is to coordinate the other agents.

The manager can:

Review the output of other agents

Decide which task should run next

Potentially reassign tasks or halt execution based on intermediate results

This is especially useful when outputs are less predictable or subjective judgment is needed—like evaluating whether a proposal is good enough before sending it on, or when the task requirements change depending on early results.

To enable hierarchical execution, you must include a manager agent in your crew.

Here's an example:

```python
manager = Agent(
    role="Project Manager",
    goal="Oversee the research and content creation
process. Validate work and ensure accuracy and
completeness.",
    backstory="A detail-oriented leader who ensures
all deliverables meet quality standards.",
    llm=llm,
    verbose=True
)

crew = Crew(
    agents=[manager, researcher, writer, editor],
    tasks=[research_task, writing_task,
editing_task],
    process=Process.hierarchical,
    verbose=True
)
```

In this setup, the `manager` agent becomes the decision-maker. They initiate the process, review the research, approve or modify the path forward, and coordinate the other agents.

One thing to note: the hierarchical handler adds complexity and cost. The manager agent reviews every stage, which leads to more LLM calls and longer execution times. But the tradeoff is higher quality, better control, and resilience to uncertainty in the workflow.

In real-world systems, hierarchical execution is ideal for:

Proposal generation with internal reviews

Research tasks requiring vetting before publication

Compliance-heavy workflows where a reviewer must sign off

Custom Process Handlers

There are use cases that neither sequential nor hierarchical processes can fully cover—such as distributed execution, retry loops, conditional branches, or smart batching. That's where **custom processes** come in.

You can define your own execution strategy by subclassing the `Process` class and implementing the `execute()` method with your desired logic.

Here's a stripped-down example of a custom process that runs only the first two tasks, logs them, and skips the rest:

```
from crewai import Process

class CustomSelectiveProcess(Process):
    def execute(self, crew):
        output_log = {}
        for task in crew.tasks[:2]:   # Only run the
first two tasks
            print(f"[CustomProcess] Running:
{task.description}")
            result = task.agent.execute_task(task)
            output_log[task.agent.role] = result
        return output_log
```

To use this custom handler:

```
crew = Crew(
    agents=[researcher, writer, editor],
    tasks=[research_task, writing_task,
editing_task],
    process=CustomSelectiveProcess(),
    verbose=True
)
```

Now you have full control over execution. You can build conditionals:

`if "error" in result:`

　`skip next task`

Or implement retry logic, where a task is rerun if output confidence is low. You can even assign tasks dynamically based on previous outputs, allowing you to rewire the entire crew's workflow mid-execution.

This is especially valuable in production systems that need more than just linear flows—like integrating human-in-the-loop checkpoints, validating against business rules, or dynamically creating new tasks from prior results.

However, with custom handlers, you also take on the responsibility of orchestration—so they should be used where structure or flexibility requirements go beyond what CrewAI provides out of the box.

Each process model—sequential, hierarchical, or custom—serves a different class of problems. Choosing the right one depends on how dependent your tasks are on one another, how confident you are in agent quality, and whether dynamic decision-making is required in the middle of execution.

When in doubt, start with sequential execution. It's the easiest to debug and reason about. Move to hierarchical when oversight is needed. Reach for custom handlers when your workflow has branching logic, retry rules, or business-specific execution conditions that can't be expressed in the standard process types.

Task Flow Logic and Orchestration Models

In a CrewAI system, your agents don't just exist independently—they carry out a sequence of tasks. How those tasks are organized, passed around, and completed depends on the **task flow logic** and the orchestration model you define. This part of system design determines whether your agents cooperate effectively or get stuck waiting on incomplete inputs, or worse, produce outputs that don't align with the expectations of downstream agents.

Understanding Task Dependencies

In CrewAI, each `Task` can specify one or more other tasks as its **context**. This means the task depends on the output of those earlier tasks and won't run until that context is available.

Think of it like this: you're designing a pipeline of data transformation steps, where each step needs the result of the previous one. But instead of working with files or function returns, you're working with autonomous agents and their outputs.

Here's a concrete setup:

```
from crewai import Task

research_task = Task(
    description="Identify and describe three
impactful AI product launches from the past 30
days.",
    expected_output="A list of three launches, each
with a short paragraph and a source link.",
    agent=researcher
)

outline_task = Task(
    description="Create a blog article outline
based on the findings from the AI product
research.",
    expected_output="A structured outline with
section headers and bullet points for key points.",
    agent=writer,
    context=[research_task]
)

draft_task = Task(
    description="Using the outline, write a full-length draft
article in Markdown.",
    expected_output="A 700-word blog post in Markdown
format.",
```

```
    agent=writer,
    context=[outline_task]
)
```

In this flow, the writer can't begin the outline task until the research task is done, and can't begin the draft until the outline is complete. This is **explicit orchestration** through task context.

Even though the same agent is executing two of the tasks, CrewAI respects the dependency order by managing execution timing behind the scenes.

Chaining Tasks with Context

The context system in CrewAI enables what's known as **task chaining**. You define this by referencing prior tasks in the `context` field. That output is then passed automatically to the next task as part of the prompt.

If you're wondering what that looks like in real execution, the content of the referenced task is injected as structured input in the prompt to the downstream agent. That gives agents visibility into previous outputs and lets them operate in a more informed, grounded way.

Here's how that plays out with another example:

Let's say you have:

A data analyst agent that extracts insights from user analytics

A designer agent that creates a design brief

A product manager agent that approves the plan

You'd set up tasks like this:

```
insight_task = Task(
    description="Analyze user engagement data and
summarize three key insights.",
    expected_output="A bulleted list with three
engagement insights, each under 50 words.",
    agent=analyst
)

design_task = Task(
```

```
    description="Based on the analytics summary,
draft a design brief that includes problem areas
and proposed UX changes.",
    expected_output="A 3-section brief: Problems,
Opportunities, and Proposed UX Solutions.",
    agent=designer,
    context=[insight_task]
)

approval_task = Task(
    description="Review the design brief and
provide approval or comments for revision.",
    expected_output="One paragraph of feedback or
approval.",
    agent=product_manager,
    context=[design_task]
)
```

This structure allows your Crew to function as a pipeline that transforms data into product design decisions, with agents working collaboratively across stages.

Controlling Flow with Conditional Logic

Sometimes you don't want every task to run by default. You may want to insert conditions: skip a task, reassign it, or modify it based on some output value. CrewAI doesn't include built-in conditional branching logic—but you can simulate this behavior with Python, or define it explicitly in a custom process handler.

Here's how you might do it manually:

```
crew.run_until(research_task)

if "no significant launches" in
research_task.output.lower():
    print("Skipping article generation due to lack
of findings.")
else:
    crew.run_from(outline_task)
```

In this pattern, you control execution based on task results, which is often necessary when real-world inputs vary in quality or volume.

For more dynamic workflows, define your own orchestration model by extending the `Process` class. This gives you full programmatic control over flow logic.

Designing for Parallel vs. Sequential Task Execution

By default, CrewAI runs tasks one at a time—either because of dependency chains or because they were defined sequentially. But if you know that certain tasks are fully independent of one another, you can run them in parallel (currently, via custom process logic).

For example, let's say:

One agent writes documentation

Another agent generates test cases

A third agent creates onboarding content

All three tasks start from the same initial system spec, and don't depend on each other. You can execute them independently to reduce latency and cost.

Here's how you might structure that:

```
doc_task = Task(..., context=[spec_task],
agent=documenter)
test_task = Task(..., context=[spec_task],
agent=test_writer)
onboard_task = Task(..., context=[spec_task],
agent=trainer)

# Custom process logic to run all three in parallel
# Or run each manually with Python threads or async
control
```

This pattern is especially helpful when scaling workflows across many documents, tickets, or content pieces.

Aggregating Outputs Across Tasks

In workflows where each task contributes a piece of a larger whole, you'll often want to **aggregate outputs**. This happens most often when you want to generate a final report or summary that references multiple earlier steps.

Here's one approach using CrewAI's task context:

```
summary_task = Task(
    description="Summarize the outcomes of the
previous three tasks into a final report for the
leadership team.",
    expected_output="A Markdown report with summary
sections and final recommendations.",
    agent=report_writer,
    context=[task1, task2, task3]
)
```

The agent receives all three outputs in one prompt, and uses that to construct a synthesized summary.

If you want tighter formatting, you can pass those task outputs into a structured JSON or Markdown template and feed that as part of the task description.

Task Routing by Role or Priority

Sometimes you need to dynamically assign tasks based on role, availability, or confidence in output. While CrewAI currently doesn't have built-in routing mechanisms like queues or load balancing, you can simulate routing by building the crew dynamically.

Let's say you want to use a different agent depending on the subject matter of the research task:

```
def select_writer(subject: str):
    if subject == "tech":
        return tech_writer
    elif subject == "finance":
        return finance_writer
    return general_writer

topic = "finance"
chosen_agent = select_writer(topic)

writing_task = Task(
```

```
    description="Write an article based on the
financial trend analysis.",
    expected_output="Markdown article under 800
words.",
    agent=chosen_agent,
    context=[trend_task]
)
```

This logic gives you the ability to customize the crew per run, which is often needed in real-world deployments where you scale up across domains or departments.

Designing a solid task flow is not just about what gets done—it's about **how** things move through your system. Well-orchestrated flows make agent outputs predictable, verifiable, and reusable. Poor orchestration leads to silent failures, overlapping work, or outputs that don't serve the downstream needs.

Real-Time Collaboration Between Agents

In CrewAI, you're not limited to sequential task assignment and one-way communication. You can design systems where agents interact with one another dynamically—sharing information, requesting clarification, negotiating task outcomes, and collaborating on shared outputs. This kind of **real-time collaboration** between agents moves you from workflow automation into true multi-agent systems.

When agents collaborate in real-time, they begin to resemble specialized team members—responding to each other's contributions and collectively solving a problem rather than just performing their individual parts in isolation. This is where CrewAI becomes much more than a prompt execution engine—it becomes a coordination platform for autonomous agents.

Setting the Foundation for Agent-to-Agent Interaction

The key to collaboration is **context passing and task referencing**, but also **prompt-level language** that encourages one agent to read, interpret, and respond to another agent's output.

Here's a practical case.

Say you're building a system where:

A **strategist agent** defines a campaign plan

A **designer agent** evaluates the visual feasibility of that plan

A **writer agent** suggests messaging based on the approved version

You want these agents to behave as if they're discussing and building toward a shared deliverable—not just working in isolation.

You'll begin by designing tasks that explicitly refer to each other's outputs. But to make this real-time and conversational, you'll also craft the task instructions to frame those outputs as something the receiving agent must read, interpret, and react to.

Building the Interaction Chain

Start by defining your agents:

```
from crewai import Agent
from langchain.chat_models import ChatOpenAI

llm = ChatOpenAI(model_name="gpt-4",
temperature=0.3)

strategist = Agent(
    role="Campaign Strategist",
    goal="Create high-level campaign plans based on
business goals.",
    backstory="You lead planning for digital
marketing initiatives across multiple platforms.",
    llm=llm,
    verbose=True
)

designer = Agent(
    role="Visual Experience Designer",
    goal="Evaluate the visual feasibility of
campaign strategies and suggest layout
improvements.",
    backstory="You ensure designs align with both
UX standards and campaign goals.",
    llm=llm,
    verbose=True
```

```
)

writer = Agent(
    role="Marketing Copywriter",
    goal="Write campaign copy that aligns with
strategic goals and approved designs.",
    backstory="You specialize in writing CTA-
focused, high-conversion messaging.",
    llm=llm,
    verbose=True
)
```

Now structure the tasks so they respond directly to one another.

Strategy Task

```
from crewai import Task

strategy_task = Task(
    description="Create a marketing campaign plan
for launching a new subscription-based note-taking
app. Include goals, target audience, and key
messages.",
    expected_output="A 3-part plan: 1) Campaign
Objectives, 2) Audience Insights, 3) Messaging
Themes.",
    agent=strategist
)
```

Design Feedback Task

The next task reacts to the first agent's output—not just consuming it, but giving structured feedback.

```
design_feedback_task = Task(
    description=(
        "Review the campaign plan created by the
strategist. Evaluate whether the key messages can
be effectively conveyed "
        "through social media graphics, web
banners, and mobile ad placements. Suggest layout
and visual approaches "
        "for each message theme."
```

```
    ),
    expected_output=(
        "A section-by-section visual feedback
summary. For each Messaging Theme, suggest a visual
treatment and highlight any issues."
    ),
    agent=designer,
    context=[strategy_task]
)
```

Here, the designer agent is behaving as if it's reacting in real-time to the strategist. You're not telling it to generate visuals—you're telling it to assess feasibility and provide design input that can guide later creative work.

Writing Task That Depends on Collaboration

The final task ties the previous two together. The writer uses both the campaign plan and the visual treatment feedback to write aligned copy.

```
writing_task = Task(
    description=(
        "Based on the strategist's plan and the
designer's feedback, write a messaging draft for a
campaign launch. "
        "Include one headline, a subhead, and a
short CTA-focused paragraph for each of the
Messaging Themes. "
        "Use language that complements the visual
direction suggested."
    ),
    expected_output="A set of labeled sections with
messaging for each visual concept.",
    agent=writer,
    context=[strategy_task, design_feedback_task]
)
```

At this point, the writer agent is behaving not like a solo content generator, but like a peer in a content team—integrating planning and design input before writing copy. That's collaborative behavior at the prompt level.

Enabling Collaborative Feedback Loops

If you want real feedback loops—where one agent critiques another's work or asks for revision—you'll structure your tasks to *invite critique and action*. This is where you simulate real-time interaction across multiple rounds.

Here's an example of an agent giving feedback:

```
feedback_task = Task(
    description=(
        "Read the campaign copy generated by the
writer. Identify any misalignment with the design
feedback or strategic goals. "
        "If everything looks good, approve it.
Otherwise, return three suggestions for
improvement."
    ),
    expected_output="A paragraph of approval or a
bullet list of changes required.",
    agent=strategist,
    context=[writing_task]
)
```

And if changes are needed, you can route them back into a second writing task that references the strategist's comments.

While this isn't synchronous in the traditional sense, it achieves real collaborative dynamics: one agent produces something, another reviews and comments, and a third acts on that review. You can link these tasks together with conditional logic or wrap them in a custom loop to keep refining outputs until you reach agreement.

Designing Collaborative Prompts

To make collaboration natural, always frame tasks as interactions. Don't just say "Write a blog post." Say:

"Review the findings from the research agent and the insights provided by the design agent. Your writing must reflect their contributions. Do not invent new arguments—summarize and align messaging instead."

This type of framing causes the LLM to respect peer input and treat previous content as authoritative, rather than generating freeform ideas.

You can even use roleplay-style prompt language to simulate conversation:

"The strategist has proposed X. The designer has raised concerns about Y. Based on both, what is the most reasonable middle ground for messaging?"

This kind of prompt lets agents reason about each other's views rather than just consume raw content.

Maintaining Output Structure for Coordination

Collaborative agents need shared standards. You'll get better results if each agent is instructed to return outputs in predictable formats that others can consume. Markdown sections, labeled bullet points, and short key-value pairs all work well.

Also, avoid overly verbose agent outputs unless you're passing them to an agent whose job is to summarize. Long, inconsistent outputs can confuse downstream agents and break coordination.

When Collaboration Works Best

You'll find this pattern is most effective in these scenarios:

Creative and editorial workflows with distinct roles (writer, editor, designer)

Strategy or planning tools where decisions evolve based on team input

Governance or policy automation where compliance, feedback, and review are needed

Any multi-agent system where validation, negotiation, or interpretation must happen between autonomous actors

This is where CrewAI's design really starts to shine—because your agents aren't just LLM endpoints. They become teammates in a structured environment.

Would you like me to continue with **Crew Communication and Output Structuring** next?

Crew Communication and Output Structuring

When multiple agents work together on complex tasks, the quality of their communication and the structure of their outputs directly impact the success of the system. In CrewAI, "communication" isn't just about passing text between agents—it's about designing workflows where each agent has enough relevant, well-formatted, and context-aware information to act intelligently.

Agents need clear inputs. Downstream agents depend on the accuracy and formatting of upstream outputs. And when agents pass results to other agents or to users, how those results are structured determines whether they're actionable, readable, or just noise.

This section focuses on two critical things:

How agents "communicate" through CrewAI's context system.

How to structure outputs so they're useful, both to humans and to other agents.

Structuring Communication Between Agents

In CrewAI, agents don't chat with each other directly in real time. Instead, communication happens through the **context** of tasks. The context field allows you to pass the output of one or more completed tasks into the prompt of another agent's task. This acts as a controlled channel of communication.

Here's a quick example of how that looks:

```
from crewai import Task

research_task = Task(
    description="Identify three key trends in
generative AI from the last 30 days, with one
credible source per trend.",
    expected_output="A Markdown list with each
trend and a source URL.",
    agent=researcher
)

analysis_task = Task(
    description="Analyze the trends identified by
the researcher. Evaluate the business impact of
each and rate them from 1 to 5.",
```

```
    expected_output="A Markdown table with columns:
Trend, Impact Summary, Rating (1-5).",
    agent=analyst,
    context=[research_task]
)
```

In this pattern, the **analyst** agent is informed by the **researcher** agent's output. This output is injected into the prompt automatically by CrewAI, preserving the full content of the previous task. The receiving agent uses that as part of its own reasoning and output generation.

This is how coordination and flow happen—each task becomes a handoff, where the next agent consumes a structured piece of content, reasons on top of it, and continues the workflow.

Writing for Other Agents (Not Just for Users)

One important mindset shift is to teach your agents to write outputs **for other agents**. That means your prompt design should steer them away from ambiguous language and toward structured, repeatable formats.

If an agent's output will be passed to another agent, don't let it output casual prose. Instead, ask for bulleted summaries, JSON, Markdown sections, or tables.

Here's an example of a well-structured output request:

```
expected_output=(
    "Return a Markdown-formatted summary with three
sections: 1) Key Findings, 2) Opportunities, 3)
Risks. "
    "Each section should contain 2-4 concise bullet
points. Avoid redundant language."
)
```

This structure gives the next agent an organized view. It doesn't need to parse or guess—it can access the correct section and respond accordingly.

Building Shared Output Conventions

If you're working with multiple agents, consistency across outputs becomes critical. Downstream agents will fail—or respond incorrectly—if the input structure changes from run to run.

Here are some strategies to maintain structure:

Use prompt constraints like: "Always return a 3-item bullet list" or "Respond in JSON format with keys: insight, source, confidence."

Review agent outputs during development to verify formatting consistency.

Use templates and placeholders to enforce response shape.

Let's say you're creating a system where multiple agents annotate a document. You want their outputs to be combined into a report later. You can enforce consistency like this:

```
expected_output=(
    "Return a JSON array of annotations. Each
annotation should include: { 'section': string,
'issue': string, 'suggestion': string }."
)
```

Then, another agent can operate on this array to make changes, summarize patterns, or classify severity levels. That's only possible because the format is structured and predictable.

Aggregating Output for Final Delivery

In many real-world CrewAI workflows, several tasks are chained together to build toward a final deliverable—a report, a document, a summary, or a decision.

In those cases, you often need a **final agent** whose job is to compile the outputs of multiple prior agents into one coherent artifact.

Here's how you'd set that up:

```
summary_task = Task(
    description="Using the research, design
feedback, and draft copy, generate a final internal
campaign brief.",
    expected_output=(
```

```
        "A Markdown document with the following
sections: 1) Strategy Summary, 2) Design Direction,
3) Messaging Draft."
    ),
    agent=editor,
    context=[research_task, design_task,
writing_task]
)
```

The **editor** agent now sees the outputs of all three previous tasks in full. You're guiding the final agent to act as the synthesizer—not creating anything new, but structuring the result for clarity and handoff.

This is especially useful in systems where the CrewAI output needs to be delivered to a stakeholder (like an email, a Google Doc, or a Slack message). Final outputs should follow the standards and structure expected by that recipient.

Designing for Human Review and Traceability

When CrewAI is used in production workflows—like content generation, internal decision support, or legal review—it's important to make the outputs easy for humans to read, review, and trace back.

That means:

Labeling each section clearly

Including references or source citations

Using formatting (like Markdown or tables) to separate parts of the output

Here's a prompt structure that encourages traceable output:

```
expected_output=(
    "Write a structured summary with these
sections:\n"
    "## Trend Overview\n<summary of the trend>\n\n"
    "## Supporting Data\n<source links and
statistics>\n\n"
    "## Recommendation\n<actionable insight based
on the trend>"
)
```

Downstream agents or human reviewers can now skim, approve, or modify specific sections. This improves transparency and trust in agent-generated content.

Handling Output Handovers Between Specialized Roles

When agents specialize—like an analyst, a summarizer, a writer, and an editor—you need each one to speak the right "language" for the next. The analyst shouldn't write in narrative prose if the summarizer needs bullet points. The summarizer shouldn't write plain text if the writer expects sectioned input.

You can design that collaboration like this:

```
summary_task = Task(
    description="Summarize the analyst's key
findings into short blurbs for the writer to use in
web content.",
    expected_output="A Markdown list with 3-5 short
blurbs, each under 30 words.",
    agent=summarizer,
    context=[analyst_task]
)

copywriting_task = Task(
    description="Turn each blurb into a website-
ready heading and supporting subhead.",
    expected_output="For each blurb, return a
'heading' and 'subhead' in JSON format.",
    agent=writer,
    context=[summary_task]
)
```

Now you've created a tightly structured handoff between agents that eliminates ambiguity.

Making Agent Output Usable by External Systems

The final step in many workflows is exporting agent output to an external system—a CMS, an API, a database, or a spreadsheet. To support that, structure output in machine-friendly formats:

JSON for structured data pipelines

Markdown for documents or web content

Plain text with delimiters if you're parsing with regex or logic

If the final output is being consumed by a human, use clear formatting. If it's being parsed by another service, constrain the agent's output format using specific instructions like:

```
"Return a valid JSON object with the following fields:
'title', 'summary', 'action_items'. Do not include
explanations or extra commentary."
```

This level of instruction prevents output from breaking downstream pipelines.

Output structure is the foundation of reliable, collaborative, and automatable AI systems. If every agent knows how to read, interpret, and build on another's output, you get a Crew that behaves like a real team—not a group of disconnected generators.

Chapter 6: Designing Real-World Workflows

In this chapter, we'll explore how to design and implement effective workflows using CrewAI. We'll focus on practical design patterns, constructing modular crews, handling errors gracefully, and examine real-world case studies to solidify our understanding.

Crew Communication and Output Structuring

In CrewAI, the effectiveness of a multi-agent system hinges on two critical aspects: how agents communicate and how their outputs are structured. Clear communication ensures that agents collaborate efficiently, while well-defined output structures guarantee that information flows seamlessly between tasks. Let's explore how to design these elements to build robust and coherent AI workflows.

Facilitating Effective Communication Between Agents

In CrewAI, agents are designed to operate not in isolation but as collaborative entities that share information and assist each other in task execution. This collaboration is fundamental to creating a cohesive system where each agent's output can serve as another's input. To achieve this, CrewAI provides mechanisms for agents to share data and delegate tasks, ensuring a dynamic and interactive workflow.

Key Strategies for Agent Communication:

Information Sharing: Agents can share data and findings with peers, ensuring that all members are well-informed and can contribute effectively.

Task Assistance: Agents have the capability to seek help from peers with the required expertise for specific tasks, promoting a cooperative environment.

Resource Allocation: Efficient distribution and sharing of resources among agents optimize task execution and overall system performance.

By implementing these strategies, agents can work together more effectively, leading to improved outcomes and a more resilient system.

Structuring Agent Outputs for Seamless Integration

The outputs of agents must be structured in a way that they can be easily interpreted and utilized by other agents or systems. CrewAI provides the TaskOutput class to encapsulate task results, supporting multiple formats such as raw strings, JSON, and Pydantic models.

Attributes of the TaskOutput Class:

Raw Output (raw): The default format, providing the unprocessed result of the task.

Pydantic Model (pydantic): A structured representation of the output using Pydantic, facilitating validation and integration.

JSON Dictionary (json_dict): The output represented as a JSON-compatible dictionary, enabling easy serialization and deserialization.

Example: Accessing Task Outputs

After executing a task, you can access its output as follows:

```
# Execute the crew
crew = Crew(
    agents=[research_agent],
    tasks=[task],
    verbose=True
)

result = crew.kickoff()

# Accessing the task output
task_output = task.output
print(f"Raw Output: {task_output.raw}")
if task_output.json_dict:
    print(f"JSON Output:
{json.dumps(task_output.json_dict, indent=2)}")
if task_output.pydantic:
    print(f"Pydantic Output:
{task_output.pydantic}")
```

This approach ensures that task outputs are consistently formatted, making them readily usable by subsequent tasks or agents.

Implementing Structured Outputs Using Pydantic Models

To enforce a specific structure on agent outputs, you can utilize Pydantic models. This method ensures that outputs adhere to a predefined schema, enhancing reliability and consistency. cite turn0 search0

Example: Defining a Pydantic Model for Task Output

```
from pydantic import BaseModel

class ResearchSummary(BaseModel):
    topic: str
    key_findings: list[str]
    references: list[str]

research_task = Task(
    description="Conduct research on the latest
advancements in renewable energy.",
    expected_output="A summary of key findings,
including references.",
    agent=research_agent,
    output_pydantic=ResearchSummary
)
```

In this example, the `ResearchSummary` model defines the expected structure of the research task's output, ensuring that the results are organized and easily interpretable by other agents or systems.

Best Practices for Output Structuring

Consistency: Maintain uniform output formats across tasks to facilitate seamless integration and reduce the likelihood of errors.

Clarity: Design outputs to be self-explanatory, minimizing the need for additional interpretation or processing.

Validation: Utilize models like Pydantic to validate outputs, ensuring they meet the required structure and content standards.

Documentation: Clearly document the expected output formats for each task, providing guidance for both developers and agents interacting with the system.

By adhering to these practices, you can create a robust framework where agents communicate effectively, and their outputs are structured to support seamless collaboration and integration.

Effective communication and structured outputs are foundational to the success of multi-agent systems in CrewAI. By implementing clear communication channels and enforcing consistent output formats, you can build systems that are not only efficient but also scalable and resilient.

Building Modular Crews

When you're developing complex AI systems, it's essential to have a structure that promotes flexibility, scalability, and maintainability. In CrewAI, this is achieved through **modular crews**—a design approach where you create distinct, interchangeable groups of agents, each responsible for specific tasks or domains. This modularity allows you to assemble, disassemble, and reassemble crews as needed, adapting to various project requirements without overhauling your entire system.

A **modular crew** consists of agents grouped based on functionality, expertise, or the nature of tasks they handle. By organizing agents into these focused units, you can manage complex workflows more effectively. Each module operates as an independent unit, capable of functioning on its own or in conjunction with other modules.

Benefits of Modular Crews:

Reusability: Modules designed for specific functions can be reused across different projects or within various parts of the same project.

Scalability: You can add or remove modules to scale your system up or down based on current needs.

Maintainability: Isolating functionalities within modules makes it easier to update or debug specific parts of the system without affecting others.

Designing Modular Crews

To build modular crews effectively, follow these steps:

Identify Core Functions: Determine the primary functions or tasks your system needs to perform.

Group Related Agents: Assign agents to modules based on shared responsibilities or the need for close collaboration.

Define Clear Interfaces: Establish how modules will communicate with each other, specifying inputs and outputs clearly.

Implement and Test Modules Independently: Develop each module separately, ensuring it performs its intended function before integrating it with others.

Integrate Modules into the Main System: Combine the modules, ensuring they work together seamlessly to achieve the overall system objectives.

Practical Example: Modular Crew for Content Creation

Let's consider a content creation pipeline where you have different modules handling various stages of the process:

Research Module: Agents responsible for gathering information on assigned topics.

Writing Module: Agents that craft articles based on the research findings.

Editing Module: Agents that review and refine the written content for clarity and accuracy.

Step 1: Define Agents for Each Module

```python
from crewai import Agent

researcher = Agent(
    role="Researcher",
    goal="Gather comprehensive information on
assigned topics.",
    backstory="An expert in conducting thorough and
efficient research across various domains."
)

writer = Agent(
    role="Writer",
    goal="Produce engaging and informative articles
based on research findings.",
```

```
    backstory="A skilled writer with a knack for
translating complex information into reader-
friendly content."
)

editor = Agent(
    role="Editor",
    goal="Review and refine articles to ensure
clarity, accuracy, and coherence.",
    backstory="A detail-oriented editor with years
of experience in polishing written content."
)
```

Step 2: Assign Tasks to Agents

```
from crewai import Task

research_task = Task(
    description="Conduct research on the latest
advancements in renewable energy.",
    expected_output="A detailed report outlining
key developments and trends in renewable energy.",
    agent=researcher
)

writing_task = Task(
    description="Write an article based on the
research report provided.",
    expected_output="A 1000-word article suitable
for publication on a tech blog.",
    agent=writer,
    context=[research_task]
)

editing_task = Task(
    description="Edit the article for grammatical
accuracy and overall readability.",
    expected_output="A polished article ready for
publication.",
    agent=editor,
    context=[writing_task]
)
```

Step 3: Assemble the Modular Crew

```
from crewai import Crew, Process

content_creation_crew = Crew(
    agents=[researcher, writer, editor],
    tasks=[research_task, writing_task,
editing_task],
    process=Process.sequential
)
```

In this setup:

The **Researcher** conducts the initial research and produces a report.

The **Writer** uses the research report to craft an article.

The **Editor** reviews and refines the article to ensure it's publication-ready.

Each module (Research, Writing, Editing) operates independently but contributes to the overall content creation process. This modular approach allows you to swap agents in and out as needed—for instance, replacing the Writer with another agent specializing in a different writing style—without disrupting the entire workflow.

Integrating Modular Crews into Larger Systems

When building larger systems, modular crews can function as building blocks. For example, if you're developing a comprehensive media production system, you might have separate crews for:

Video Production: Handling scripting, filming, and editing of video content.

Graphic Design: Creating visual assets for various media.

Content Distribution: Managing the dissemination of content across platforms.

Each of these crews operates independently but can be integrated to work together, providing a flexible and scalable system architecture.

Building modular crews in CrewAI allows you to create flexible, scalable, and maintainable AI systems. By grouping agents into focused modules, you can manage complex workflows more effectively, reuse components across projects, and adapt to changing requirements with ease. This approach not only streamlines development but also enhances the robustness of your AI solutions.

Error Handling and Recovery

In any real-world software system, things will eventually go wrong. And CrewAI workflows are no exception. Whether it's a malformed API response, a failed model call, invalid output from an agent, or simply a logic error in task sequencing—if your system doesn't know how to handle failure gracefully, it won't be dependable enough for production.

That's why building robust **error handling and recovery** into your CrewAI architecture is not optional—it's critical.

Before you can build proper recovery strategies, you need to know where and why things typically fail. The most common failure points include:

The LLM response from an agent is incomplete or empty

A tool raises an exception (e.g., API not responding, bad input)

The output format of a task is not structured as expected (e.g., invalid JSON)

A dependency task fails, breaking the flow for a downstream task

Your crew orchestration logic (e.g., a custom process) encounters a logic or type error

Each of these issues can be caught and handled with code—but only if you're designing your crews to inspect, log, and react to what's going on inside them.

Wrapping Agent Calls in Try/Except Blocks

When you run a crew or an agent task individually, any failure in the tool or LLM chain will typically raise an exception or return None. You should always catch this early and log enough detail to diagnose the problem.

Here's an example of manually executing a task with error handling:

```
from crewai import Crew

try:
```

```
    result = crew.run()
except Exception as e:
    print(f" X  Crew execution failed: {str(e)}")
    # Optional: write to a log file or alert system
```

If you're debugging a single agent's task:

```
try:
    output = agent.execute_task(task)
except Exception as e:
    print(f" X  Agent {agent.role} failed: {e}")
```

These exception handlers give you a hook to prevent total system failure and take an alternate path when needed.

Validating and Retrying Task Outputs

Sometimes the agent produces an output, but it's not what you expect. Maybe you asked for a JSON object, and it returned plain text. Or it gave you a paragraph when you needed a table.

In these cases, the error isn't a crash—it's a content failure. To catch these, inspect the output before moving to the next task.

Let's define a simple validation function:

```
def validate_json_structure(output: str,
required_keys: list[str]) -> bool:
    import json
    try:
        data = json.loads(output)
        return all(key in data for key in
required_keys)
    except Exception:
        return False
```

Use this after a task completes:

```
task_result = agent.execute_task(task)

if not validate_json_structure(task_result,
["summary", "recommendation"]):
    print(" ⚠ Invalid structure. Retrying...")
```

```
        task_result = agent.execute_task(task)  # Retry
once
```

You can even wrap this in a retry loop with backoff logic:

```
import time

def retry_task(agent, task, retries=3, delay=2):
    for attempt in range(retries):
        try:
            result = agent.execute_task(task)
            if result:
                return result
        except Exception as e:
            print(f"Attempt {attempt+1} failed:
{e}")
        time.sleep(delay)
    return None
```

This gives your system resilience without turning individual failures into total process halts.

Checking for Empty or Unusable Outputs

CrewAI doesn't always throw exceptions if an agent gives a weak output. The LLM may technically respond with something, but it might not be useful. Always check if the result meets your quality bar.

Example:

```
result = agent.execute_task(task)

if result is None or len(result.strip()) < 20:
    print(f"⚠ Output too short or empty from
{agent.role}")
    # Optionally: assign fallback agent or escalate
```

This kind of guard lets you insert quality checks before blindly passing data to the next agent in the crew.

Creating Fallback Agents

Another practical strategy is to have multiple agents available for the same role—especially if one fails or produces poor results. This is useful for redundancy.

Example:

```
from random import choice

agents = [primary_writer, backup_writer]

for agent in agents:
    try:
        result = agent.execute_task(task)
        if result:
            break
    except:
        continue
```

You can even create a meta-agent that chooses the best result between multiple attempts or merges them into a better final draft.

Logging for Debugging and Auditing

When running production crews, always log each task's output, errors, and timestamps so you can diagnose failures after the fact.

Use the built-in `verbose=True` setting on the `Crew` and `Agent` objects during development, and switch to custom logging in production:

```
import logging

logging.basicConfig(filename="crew_log.txt",
level=logging.INFO)

def safe_task_run(agent, task):
    try:
        result = agent.execute_task(task)
        logging.info(f"{agent.role} completed task:
{task.description}")
        return result
    except Exception as e:
        logging.error(f"{agent.role} failed on
task: {task.description} - {str(e)}")
```

135

```
        return None
```

Handling Task Failure Without Crashing the Crew

If you're using `Crew.run()` with a sequence of tasks, one failure might break the whole pipeline. To avoid this, handle errors inside a custom process:

```python
from crewai import Process

class SafeSequentialProcess(Process):
    def execute(self, crew):
        results = {}
        for task in crew.tasks:
            try:
                result =
task.agent.execute_task(task)
                task.output = result
                results[task.agent.role] = result
            except Exception as e:
                results[task.agent.role] = f"ERROR:
{str(e)}"
                # Optionally assign a backup task
or log
        return results
```

Now you can run your crew with:

```python
crew = Crew(
    agents=[researcher, writer],
    tasks=[research_task, writing_task],
    process=SafeSequentialProcess()
)
crew.run()
```

This ensures the system always finishes execution and provides full visibility into what worked and what didn't.

Summary of Defensive Design

These techniques together create a defensible system:

Use `try/except` for any direct calls to agents

Validate outputs before passing them downstream

Use retry loops with limits

Build fallback roles into your crew

Structure task outputs clearly (Markdown, JSON, etc.)

Log everything for traceability

A CrewAI system without failure handling is only as strong as its weakest agent. But a system designed for recovery becomes something you can trust to run unsupervised—and eventually, something you can scale.

Case Study: Building a Content Automation Workflow

In today's fast-paced digital environment, producing high-quality content consistently is a significant challenge for many organizations. Automating the content creation process not only enhances efficiency but also ensures a steady stream of engaging material for audiences. In this case study, we'll explore how to build a content automation workflow using CrewAI, a platform designed to orchestrate multiple AI agents collaborating to perform complex tasks. cite turn0 search0

CrewAI is a framework that enables developers to build and deploy automated workflows using multiple AI agents that collaborate to perform complex tasks. It allows for the creation of specialized agents, each with distinct roles and objectives, working together to achieve a common goal.

Key Components of CrewAI:

Agents: Autonomous units with specific roles, goals, and backstories. They can perform tasks, make decisions, and communicate with other agents.

Tasks: Units of work assigned to agents, each with a description and expected output.

Crew: A collection of agents and tasks that work together to execute a process.

Designing the Content Automation Workflow

The goal is to automate the creation of blog articles on various topics. The workflow involves three primary agents: a Content Planner, a Content Writer, and an Editor. Each agent has a specific role in the content creation process.

1. Content Planner:

Role: Develops a comprehensive plan for the blog article, including an outline, target audience analysis, and SEO keywords.

Goal: Ensure the content aligns with current trends and audience interests.

Backstory: An experienced strategist adept at identifying relevant topics and structuring content effectively.

2. Content Writer:

Role: Crafts the blog post based on the planner's outline, incorporating engaging language and adhering to the proposed structure.

Goal: Produce informative and captivating content that resonates with readers.

Backstory: A skilled writer with a knack for translating complex ideas into reader-friendly material.

3. Editor:

Role: Reviews and refines the written content to ensure clarity, coherence, and grammatical accuracy.

Goal: Maintain a high standard of quality and consistency across all published articles.

Backstory: A detail-oriented editor with years of experience in polishing written content.

Implementing the Workflow with CrewAI

To bring this workflow to life, we'll define each agent and their corresponding tasks using CrewAI's framework.

Step 1: Define the Agents

```
from crewai import Agent
from langchain.chat_models import import ChatOpenAI
```

```python
# Initialize the language model
llm = ChatOpenAI(model_name="gpt-4",
temperature=0.3)

# Content Planner Agent
planner = Agent(
    role="Content Planner",
    goal="Develop comprehensive plans for blog
articles on various topics.",
    backstory="An experienced strategist adept at
identifying relevant topics and structuring content
effectively.",
    llm=llm,
    verbose=True
)

# Content Writer Agent
writer = Agent(
    role="Content Writer",
    goal="Craft engaging and informative blog posts
based on provided outlines.",
    backstory="A skilled writer with a knack for
translating complex ideas into reader-friendly
material.",
    llm=llm,
    verbose=True
)

# Editor Agent
editor = Agent(
    role="Editor",
    goal="Review and refine written content to
ensure clarity, coherence, and grammatical
accuracy.",
    backstory="A detail-oriented editor with years
of experience in polishing written content.",
    llm=llm,
    verbose=True
)
```

Step 2: Assign Tasks to Agents

```
from crewai import Task

# Task for Content Planner
planning_task = Task(
    description="Develop a content plan for a blog
article on the assigned topic, including an
outline, target audience analysis, and SEO
keywords.",
    expected_output="A detailed content plan
document with an outline, audience analysis, and
SEO keywords.",
    agent=planner
)

# Task for Content Writer
writing_task = Task(
    description="Write a blog post based on the
content plan provided by the planner.",
    expected_output="A well-crafted blog article
adhering to the provided outline and incorporating
SEO keywords.",
    agent=writer,
    context=[planning_task]
)

# Task for Editor
editing_task = Task(
    description="Review and edit the blog post to
ensure clarity, coherence, and grammatical
accuracy.",
    expected_output="A polished and publication-
ready blog article.",
    agent=editor,
    context=[writing_task]
)
```

Step 3: Assemble the Crew and Execute the Workflow

```
from crewai import Crew, Process

# Assemble the crew with the defined agents and
tasks
content_creation_crew = Crew(
```

```
    agents=[planner, writer, editor],
    tasks=[planning_task, writing_task,
editing_task],
    process=Process.sequential,
    verbose=True
)

# Execute the workflow
result =
content_creation_crew.kickoff(inputs={"topic":
"Artificial Intelligence"})
print(result)
```

Real-World Application and Benefits

Implementing this automated content creation workflow offers several advantages:

Efficiency: Streamlines the content creation process, reducing the time required to produce high-quality articles.

Consistency: Ensures a uniform standard of quality and style across all content.

Scalability: Facilitates the production of a larger volume of content without a proportional increase in resources.

For instance, a digital marketing agency can utilize this workflow to generate blog posts on diverse topics, maintaining a consistent publishing schedule and engaging their target audience effectively.

By leveraging CrewAI to build a content automation workflow, organizations can enhance their content production capabilities, ensuring efficiency, consistency, and scalability. This approach not only meets the demands of a dynamic digital landscape but also positions organizations to deliver valuable content to their audiences continuously. □

Case Study: Research + Analysis + Reporting Crew

One of the most practical applications of multi-agent systems is automating structured decision-making workflows—particularly when that workflow requires research, interpretation of findings, and generation of reports. Whether you're preparing a competitive analysis, summarizing regulatory updates, or compiling product feedback into actionable summaries, CrewAI can help you create repeatable systems that do this with precision and scale.

This case study walks you through building a fully functional, modular CrewAI system designed to perform real-world research, synthesize insights, and deliver final reports in a clear, human-readable format. The agents involved will each take ownership of a core stage in the workflow—research, analysis, and reporting—passing context between them in a clean, traceable chain.

Defining the Goal

You're tasked with building a system that can:

Research the current state of a specific market

Extract meaningful patterns or opportunities from the research

Create a report that presents those insights clearly to stakeholders

For the sake of this case, the topic is **"AI-powered productivity tools for remote teams."**

You want the output to be structured as a professional-grade business report, including an executive summary, a breakdown of key players, trends, risks, and recommendations.

Designing the Agents

We'll define three specialized agents:

A **Research Analyst** to perform live information gathering using tools

A **Strategy Analyst** to interpret the research and find business-relevant insights

A **Report Writer** to organize the insights into a final executive document

Let's start by defining the agents in CrewAI.

```
from crewai import Agent
from langchain.chat_models import ChatOpenAI
```

```
llm = ChatOpenAI(model_name="gpt-4",
temperature=0.3)

researcher = Agent(
    role="Research Analyst",
    goal="Collect and organize up-to-date
information about the target market.",
    backstory="A skilled analyst with expertise in
gathering competitive intelligence and technical
product data.",
    llm=llm,
    verbose=True
)

strategist = Agent(
    role="Strategy Analyst",
    goal="Interpret research findings and identify
actionable insights.",
    backstory="A data-driven strategist who turns
qualitative research into decision frameworks.",
    llm=llm,
    verbose=True
)

writer = Agent(
    role="Business Report Writer",
    goal="Draft clear, structured, and polished
reports for executive-level review.",
    backstory="An experienced writer who
communicates strategic findings to non-technical
stakeholders.",
    llm=llm,
    verbose=True
)
```

Defining the Tasks

Each task is designed to correspond to one stage of the process and references the necessary upstream context.

```
from crewai import Task
```

```python
research_task = Task(
    description=(
        "Conduct comprehensive market research on
AI-powered productivity tools for remote teams. "
        "Identify at least 5 relevant products or
companies, summarize their core features, and note
any recent developments."
    ),
    expected_output=(
        "A Markdown document listing each product
or company, their main features, target users,
pricing model, and recent announcements."
    ),
    agent=researcher
)

analysis_task = Task(
    description=(
        "Using the market research, identify
current trends, unmet needs, and potential growth
areas in the space of AI-powered productivity
tools. "
        "Prioritize findings that are relevant to
mid-size SaaS teams working remotely."
    ),
    expected_output=(
        "A structured summary with sections for:
Trends, Opportunities, Risks, and Recommendations."
    ),
    agent=strategist,
    context=[research_task]
)

report_task = Task(
    description=(
        "Write a professional report titled 'Market
Outlook: AI Productivity Tools for Remote Teams'. "
        "Use the analysis findings and research to
generate an executive summary, followed by the full
findings."
    ),
    expected_output=(
```

```
         "A Markdown-formatted report with: 1.
Executive Summary (1 paragraph), 2. Market
Overview, 3. Strategic Insights, and 4. Final
Recommendations."
    ),
    agent=writer,
    context=[analysis_task, research_task]
)
```

This structure allows outputs to cascade cleanly from one stage to the next.
The researcher provides the data, the strategist interprets it, and the writer
formalizes it.

Executing the Workflow

To execute the workflow, you assemble the crew using the sequential
execution process.

```
from crewai import Crew, Process

crew = Crew(
    agents=[researcher, strategist, writer],
    tasks=[research_task, analysis_task,
report_task],
    process=Process.sequential,
    verbose=True
)

result = crew.kickoff()
print(result)
```

When you run this script, the `research_task` is completed first, generating a
structured Markdown summary of the market. That output becomes part of the
prompt for the `analysis_task`, which identifies business-relevant takeaways.
The result of the analysis, along with the research, is then passed into the
`report_task`, producing the final document.

What Makes This Approach Practical

There are a few reasons this crew structure works well in the real world:

Each agent's task is clearly scoped and avoids overlapping responsibilities

145

Task outputs are structured in Markdown, making them easy to format, render, or export

You can reuse or extend any task individually—for example, running just the analysis if new data arrives

It's easy to replace agents—for example, swapping the writer with a translator if the output needs to be localized

You can also extend this crew to run on a schedule, write multiple versions of the report for different audiences, or generate visuals by inserting a design agent after the writing stage.

Validating Results and Ensuring Reliability

To ensure the outputs are structured and usable, validate them after each stage. Here's a sample post-task check:

```
if "Trends" not in analysis_task.output:
    raise ValueError("Missing expected section:
Trends")

if "Executive Summary" not in report_task.output:
    print("⚠ Report missing summary. Consider
rerunning the report task.")
```

You can also use the `.json_dict` or `.pydantic` fields if your output is structured via JSON or models.

Real-World Extension Example

A consulting firm might use this exact architecture to automate competitive landscape reports for clients. The only input would be the topic—say, "AI note-taking apps"—and the crew would output a full report suitable for executive briefing decks.

By scheduling this crew to run weekly, they could deliver consistently fresh insights with minimal manual work, freeing consultants to focus on advising rather than compiling.

This kind of modular, focused, multi-agent crew is one of the most scalable patterns in CrewAI development. Each agent handles a domain of responsibility, and together they replicate the behavior of a skilled analyst team working toward a shared outcome.

Chapter 7: Advanced Control and Customization

As your CrewAI projects grow in complexity, you'll start running into situations where the built-in orchestration options—like `Process.sequential` or `Process.hierarchical`—just don't give you the control you need. Maybe you want to make decisions in the middle of a workflow. Maybe tasks need to repeat, fork, branch, or adapt based on changing context. Or maybe your agents need to keep track of state over multiple interactions across days or even weeks.

This chapter introduces you to the tools you'll need to solve those problems: custom process handlers, conditionals, event-driven coordination, persistent state, and long-lived agents.

Custom Process Handlers

Imagine you're orchestrating a team of AI agents to conduct a comprehensive market analysis. The workflow involves multiple stages: data collection, data analysis, report drafting, and final review. In a standard sequential process, each task would be executed one after the other. However, what if the data analysis stage requires inputs from multiple data collection tasks running concurrently? Or perhaps the final review should only be triggered if certain quality thresholds are met in the report drafting stage. These complex workflows necessitate a level of control that default process handlers may not provide.

By creating a custom process handler, you can implement logic that manages these intricacies, ensuring tasks are executed in the desired order, under the right conditions, and with the appropriate dependencies.

Implementing a Custom Process Handler

To create a custom process handler in CrewAI, you'll need to subclass the `Process` class and override its `execute` method. This method is where you'll define the logic for task execution, including task sequencing, concurrency, conditional execution, and error handling.

Here's a step-by-step guide to implementing a custom process handler:

Subclass the `Process` Class: Begin by creating a new class that inherits from `Process`.

Override the `execute` Method: Within your subclass, define the `execute` method, which will contain the logic for managing task execution.

Implement Task Execution Logic: Within the `execute` method, write the code that assigns tasks to agents, determines the order of execution, handles task dependencies, and manages any conditional logic.

Handle Outputs and Errors: Ensure that the `execute` method appropriately handles task outputs and includes error handling to manage any issues that arise during task execution.

Practical Example: Parallel Data Collection with Conditional Analysis

Let's consider a practical example where we need to collect data from multiple sources concurrently, analyze the aggregated data, and then generate a report only if the analysis meets certain criteria.

Here's how you might implement this using a custom process handler:

```python
from crewai import Process, Task, Agent

class CustomMarketAnalysisProcess(Process):
    def execute(self, crew):
        # Step 1: Concurrent Data Collection
        data_sources = ['Source A', 'Source B',
'Source C']
        collection_tasks = []
        for source in data_sources:
            task = Task(description=f"Collect data
from {source}",
agent=crew.get_agent('DataCollector'))
            collection_tasks.append(task)
            task.agent.execute_task(task)

        # Step 2: Data Analysis (only if all data
collection tasks succeed)
        if all(task.output for task in
collection_tasks):
```

```
            analysis_task =
Task(description="Analyze collected data",
agent=crew.get_agent('DataAnalyst'))
            analysis_result =
analysis_task.agent.execute_task(analysis_task)

            # Step 3: Report Generation (only if
analysis meets criteria)
            if 'significant findings' in
analysis_result:
                report_task =
Task(description="Generate market analysis report",
agent=crew.get_agent('ReportWriter'))

report_task.agent.execute_task(report_task)
            else:
                print("Analysis did not yield
significant findings. Report generation skipped.")
        else:
            print("Data collection failed for one
or more sources. Analysis and report generation
skipped.")
```

In this example:

Concurrent Data Collection: Data collection tasks are initiated for multiple sources simultaneously.

Conditional Data Analysis: The analysis task is executed only if all data collection tasks are successful.

Conditional Report Generation: The report is generated only if the analysis yields significant findings.

This custom process handler ensures that each stage of the workflow is executed based on the success of the preceding tasks, providing a robust and efficient workflow tailored to the specific needs of the market analysis project.

Real-World Application: Financial Data Processing

Consider a financial services firm that needs to process data from various stock exchanges to generate daily market summaries. The firm can implement a custom process handler to:

Fetch Data Concurrently: Collect stock data from multiple exchanges simultaneously to ensure timely information.

Validate Data Integrity: Check the collected data for completeness and accuracy before proceeding.

Analyze Market Trends: Perform analyses to identify significant market movements or trends.

Generate Reports Conditionally: Produce market summaries only if notable trends are detected, optimizing resource usage.

By customizing the process handler, the firm can ensure that its data processing pipeline is both efficient and responsive to the dynamic nature of financial markets.

Custom process handlers in CrewAI provide the flexibility to design workflows that meet complex and specific requirements. By subclassing the `Process` class and implementing tailored execution logic, you can control task sequencing, concurrency, conditional execution, and error handling to suit your project's needs. This level of customization empowers you to build sophisticated AI agent collaborations that operate seamlessly within your defined parameters, enhancing the efficiency and effectiveness of your automated workflows.

Implementing Conditional Logic in Crews

In complex workflows, it's often necessary to make decisions based on the outcomes of previous tasks. This is where implementing conditional logic within your CrewAI crews becomes essential. By incorporating conditions, you can create dynamic and responsive workflows that adapt to varying scenarios, ensuring that each task is executed only when appropriate.

Conditional logic allows your crew to evaluate specific conditions and decide the subsequent course of action based on those evaluations. This means tasks can be executed, skipped, or repeated depending on the outcomes of prior tasks or the state of the system. Implementing such logic enhances the flexibility and efficiency of your AI-driven processes.

Implementing Conditional Tasks

CrewAI provides a specialized class called `ConditionalTask` that facilitates the incorporation of conditional logic into your workflows. A `ConditionalTask` operates like a regular task but includes an additional `condition` parameter—a function that determines whether the task should be executed based on the output of a preceding task.

Here's how you can define and use a `ConditionalTask`:

Define the Condition Function: Create a function that evaluates the output of a prior task and returns a boolean value indicating whether the subsequent task should proceed.

Set Up Agents: Define the agents responsible for executing the tasks.

Create Tasks and Conditional Tasks: Establish the tasks, including the conditional tasks, specifying their descriptions, expected outputs, assigned agents, and the condition functions.

Assemble the Crew: Combine the agents and tasks into a crew and initiate the workflow.

Practical Example: Data Collection and Analysis

Consider a scenario where you need to collect data about events in San Francisco, process the data to ensure completeness, and generate a summary report. If the initial data collection yields fewer than 10 events, additional data collection should be triggered.

Here's how you can implement this workflow:

```
from typing import List
from pydantic import BaseModel
from crewai import Agent, Crew
from crewai.tasks.conditional_task import
ConditionalTask
from crewai.tasks.task_output import TaskOutput
from crewai.task import Task
from crewai_tools import SerperDevTool

# Define a condition function for the conditional
task
def is_data_incomplete(output: TaskOutput) -> bool:
```

```python
        return len(output.pydantic.events) < 10

# Define the agents
data_fetcher = Agent(
    role="Data Fetcher",
    goal="Fetch data online using Serper tool",
    backstory="An expert in retrieving online event
data.",
    verbose=True,
    tools=[SerperDevTool()]
)

data_processor = Agent(
    role="Data Processor",
    goal="Process fetched data",
    backstory="Specializes in data validation and
enrichment.",
    verbose=True
)

summary_generator = Agent(
    role="Summary Generator",
    goal="Generate summary from fetched data",
    backstory="Experienced in creating
comprehensive event summaries.",
    verbose=True
)

# Define the expected output model
class EventOutput(BaseModel):
    events: List[str]

# Define the tasks
fetch_data_task = Task(
    description="Fetch data about events in San
Francisco using Serper tool",
    expected_output="List of events in SF this
week",
    agent=data_fetcher,
    output_pydantic=EventOutput,
)
```

```
conditional_fetch_task = ConditionalTask(
    description="Fetch additional events to ensure
at least 10 events are available.",
    expected_output="An updated list of at least 10
events in SF this week",
    condition=is_data_incomplete,
    agent=data_processor,
)

generate_summary_task = Task(
    description="Generate a summary of events in
San Francisco from the fetched data",
    expected_output="A comprehensive report on
events in SF this week",
    agent=summary_generator,
)

# Assemble the crew
event_analysis_crew = Crew(
    agents=[data_fetcher, data_processor,
summary_generator],
    tasks=[fetch_data_task, conditional_fetch_task,
generate_summary_task],
    process=Process.sequential
)

# Execute the crew
result = event_analysis_crew.kickoff()
```

In this example:

Initial Data Collection: The `fetch_data_task` retrieves event data for San Francisco.

Conditional Additional Data Collection: The `conditional_fetch_task` checks if the number of events is less than 10 using the `is_data_incomplete` function. If so, it triggers additional data collection to meet the required number of events.

Summary Generation: Finally, the `generate_summary_task` compiles the collected data into a comprehensive report.

This workflow ensures that the summary report is based on a complete set of event data, enhancing its usefulness and accuracy.

Real-World Application: Customer Support Automation

In a customer support system, implementing conditional logic can streamline operations and improve response times. For instance, an AI agent can first attempt to resolve a customer query using a knowledge base. If the confidence level in the provided solution is below a certain threshold, the system can automatically escalate the issue to a human representative. This approach ensures that customers receive accurate information promptly while reserving human intervention for more complex issues.

Integrating conditional logic into your CrewAI workflows empowers your AI agents to make informed decisions, resulting in more dynamic and efficient processes. By utilizing `ConditionalTask` and defining clear condition functions, you can create workflows that adapt to varying situations, ensuring that each task is executed appropriately based on the context. This capability is invaluable in developing sophisticated AI-driven systems that can handle complex, real-world scenarios effectively.

Event-Based and Goal-Oriented Coordination

In complex AI workflows, especially those involving multiple agents, the ability to coordinate tasks effectively is crucial. CrewAI offers robust mechanisms for event-based and goal-oriented coordination, allowing agents to respond dynamically to events and align their actions toward overarching objectives.

Event-based coordination enables agents to react to specific occurrences or "events" during workflow execution. This approach allows for dynamic and responsive systems where agents can adjust their behavior based on real-time inputs or changes in the environment.

In CrewAI, this is facilitated through an event-driven architecture where events are emitted at various stages of task execution. Developers can create custom event listeners to handle these events, executing specific actions when certain conditions are met.

Implementing Custom Event Listeners

To implement event-based coordination, you can create custom event listeners that respond to specific events emitted during the crew's operation. Here's how you can set up a custom event listener in CrewAI:

```python
from crewai.utilities.events import (
    CrewKickoffStartedEvent,
    AgentExecutionCompletedEvent,
)
from crewai.utilities.events.base_event_listener
import BaseEventListener

class CustomEventListener(BaseEventListener):
    def setup_listeners(self, crewai_event_bus):

@crewai_event_bus.on(CrewKickoffStartedEvent)
        def on_crew_started(source, event):
            print(f"Crew '{event.crew_name}' has
started execution.")


@crewai_event_bus.on(AgentExecutionCompletedEvent)
        def on_agent_execution_completed(source,
event):
            print(f"Agent '{event.agent.role}'
completed task with output: {event.output}")

# Instantiate the listener
custom_listener = CustomEventListener()
```

In this example, the `CustomEventListener` class listens for the `CrewKickoffStartedEvent` and `AgentExecutionCompletedEvent`. When these events are emitted, the corresponding methods are triggered, allowing you to insert custom logic or monitoring as needed. cite turn0 search5

Goal-Oriented Coordination

Goal-oriented coordination focuses on aligning the actions of various agents toward a shared objective. Each agent operates with an understanding of the overall goal, enabling collaborative efforts that are coherent and efficient.

Defining Agent Goals

In CrewAI, each agent is assigned a specific role and goal, which guides its behavior and decision-making processes. Clearly defining these goals ensures that all agents are working synergistically toward the crew's mission.

Coordinating Tasks Toward Goals

Tasks are structured to contribute directly to the overarching goal. By sequencing tasks appropriately and assigning them to agents whose roles align with the task requirements, you create a streamlined workflow that progresses logically toward the desired outcome.

Example: Collaborative Report Generation

Consider a scenario where a team of agents is tasked with generating a comprehensive market analysis report. The goal is to produce an insightful document that informs strategic decisions.

Research Analyst Agent: Gathers relevant market data.

Data Analyst Agent: Processes and interprets the collected data to identify trends.

Report Writer Agent: Compiles the analyzed data into a structured report.

Each agent's tasks are coordinated to ensure that the output of one serves as the input for the next, all aligned toward the goal of creating the market analysis report.

Integrating Event-Based and Goal-Oriented Approaches

Combining event-based and goal-oriented coordination allows for the creation of adaptive and purpose-driven AI systems. Agents can respond to real-time events while maintaining focus on their collective objectives, resulting in workflows that are both flexible and goal-focused.☐

Practical Implementation

To integrate these approaches, you can set up event listeners that monitor for specific triggers and adjust agent tasks or priorities accordingly, all within the framework of the crew's goals. This ensures that while agents are responsive to immediate events, their actions remain aligned with the overall mission.

Example: Real-Time Data Monitoring System

Imagine a system where agents monitor live data feeds to detect significant market changes and generate alerts or reports.

Event Listener: Monitors data feeds for predefined thresholds or patterns.

Alert Agent: Triggered by the event listener to notify stakeholders of significant changes.

Analysis Agent: Conducts a deeper analysis of the event and prepares a detailed report.

In this setup, the event listener ensures that agents react promptly to market changes, while the agents' tasks are structured to provide meaningful insights, all contributing to the goal of informed decision-making.

By leveraging CrewAI's capabilities for event-based and goal-oriented coordination, you can design AI systems that are both responsive to real-time events and aligned with strategic objectives. This dual approach enhances the effectiveness and adaptability of your AI workflows, enabling them to handle complex tasks with greater efficiency.

Long-Running Agent Sessions

By default, CrewAI agents operate statelessly. Each time you call an agent to execute a task, it processes the input independently—without knowledge of any previous actions unless that context is passed explicitly in the prompt. This is efficient for one-off operations, but many real-world use cases require continuity over time. In these scenarios, your agents need to retain memory, manage evolving context, and interact with users or other agents over extended periods.

A long-running session gives an agent the ability to persist its memory, conversation history, and goals beyond a single task or crew run. This pattern is essential for use cases like customer support, project management, virtual assistants, research bots, and any task that unfolds incrementally across time.

To build long-running sessions with CrewAI, you need to manage persistent state explicitly. That includes tracking conversation history, storing outputs, and providing continuity between interactions—even across separate script executions or HTTP calls.

Preserving Agent Memory Across Runs

At the core of a long-running session is memory. This memory can take many forms: full transcripts, extracted facts, key-value metadata, or even structured domain models. Whatever format you choose, the memory must be:

Stored somewhere reliable (e.g., database, local file, Redis)

Restored when a session resumes

Injected into the prompt or context of the agent

Let's use a simple example using an in-memory Python structure. Later, you'll see how to persist it across restarts.

First, define a reusable memory container:

```python
class AgentMemory:
    def __init__(self):
        self.history = []

    def add_entry(self, user_input, agent_output):
        self.history.append({
            "user_input": user_input,
            "agent_output": agent_output
        })

    def build_context(self):
        return "\n".join([
            f"User: {entry['user_input']}\nAgent: {entry['agent_output']}"
            for entry in self.history
        ])
```

Now wrap your agent so that it uses this context on every new task.

```python
from crewai import Agent

class SessionAgent:
    def __init__(self, agent: Agent, memory: AgentMemory):
```

```python
        self.agent = agent
        self.memory = memory

    def execute_with_memory(self, new_prompt: str):
        full_prompt = self.memory.build_context() +
f"\nUser: {new_prompt}"
        task = {
            "description": full_prompt,
            "agent": self.agent
        }
        result = self.agent.execute_task(task)
        self.memory.add_entry(new_prompt, result)
        return result
```

You now have an agent that remembers its conversation history and uses it to inform future outputs.

Persisting the Session

To make this agent reusable across multiple sessions or API calls, the memory object must be stored externally. Let's use a basic file-based approach to persist it using JSON.

```python
import json
import os

class PersistentAgentMemory(AgentMemory):
    def __init__(self, session_id):
        self.session_id = session_id
        self.file_path =
f"sessions/{session_id}.json"
        self.history = self._load()

    def _load(self):
        if os.path.exists(self.file_path):
            with open(self.file_path, "r") as f:
                return json.load(f)
        return []

    def save(self):
        with open(self.file_path, "w") as f:
            json.dump(self.history, f, indent=2)
```

```
def add_entry(self, user_input, agent_output):
    super().add_entry(user_input, agent_output)
    self.save()
```

Now the agent will resume with the same context even after being restarted:

```
session_id = "client_123"
memory =
PersistentAgentMemory(session_id=session_id)
session_agent = SessionAgent(agent, memory)

result = session_agent.execute_with_memory("What
should I focus on next week?")
print(result)
```

This method enables you to scale agents across multiple users or projects—each with their own persistent memory state.

Real-World Example: Project Manager Agent

Let's say you're building a virtual project manager that helps a team plan weekly work. Each team has an agent. Every interaction updates the shared memory.

```
team_agent =
SessionAgent(agent=project_manager_agent,
memory=PersistentAgentMemory("team_alpha"))

team_agent.execute_with_memory("We completed the
feature rollout.")
team_agent.execute_with_memory("Plan tasks for next
sprint.")
team_agent.execute_with_memory("Add documentation
and a test plan.")
```

Because the memory is preserved between requests, the agent's suggestions will evolve based on what's already happened, what was already planned, and what needs follow-up.

You could connect this to a frontend UI, Slack bot, or REST API and give each team their own long-lived intelligent assistant.

Managing and Querying Long-Term Context

161

As the memory grows, you may need more structure and querying ability. Consider storing structured JSON per interaction:

```
{
   "user_input": "Start the feature freeze today",
   "agent_output": "Acknowledged. Feature freeze
begins today. Informing the QA team."
}
```

Store this in a NoSQL database like MongoDB or Firebase so that you can:

Query past events by keyword or date

Filter interactions by type (e.g., decisions, confirmations, questions)

Limit context injection to the most recent 5–10 entries for prompt efficiency

This is essential if your long-running sessions span weeks or months. You don't want to include all historical entries on every interaction, but you may want to refer to them for validation or backtracking.

Design Considerations for Long-Running Agents

Here are some best practices you'll want to consider when designing long-lived sessions:

Inject memory selectively. Don't overload every prompt. Focus on relevant history only.

Limit session memory per interaction. GPT models have context length limits. Slice intelligently.

Store summaries as well as raw interactions. You may want to periodically compress memory.

Enable logging. Long sessions often require traceability and auditability.

Handle memory corruption or edge cases gracefully. Always validate memory before injecting.

A long-running agent isn't just one that keeps answering questions. It's an agent that **learns**, **remembers**, and **adapts** based on what's already happened. Whether you're building an executive assistant, a research agent, or a support system, long-lived memory is what gives your system continuity and intelligence beyond one-off calls.

Integrating State and Persistence

In complex AI workflows, managing state and ensuring data persistence are crucial for creating systems that are both reliable and capable of handling long-term tasks. CrewAI offers robust mechanisms to maintain state across various operations and persist critical information, enabling the development of sophisticated and resilient AI applications.

Understanding State in CrewAI

State refers to the current data and context that an AI system holds during its operation. Effective state management allows agents to remember previous interactions, make informed decisions based on past data, and maintain continuity throughout a workflow. In CrewAI, state can be managed using unstructured or structured approaches, each offering different levels of flexibility and control.

Unstructured State Management

Unstructured state management employs a dictionary-like object to store and modify data. This method provides flexibility, allowing developers to add or change state information dynamically. However, it may lack the rigor needed for complex applications where data validation and consistency are critical.

Structured State Management

Structured state management utilizes models, such as those provided by Pydantic, to define a clear schema for the state. This approach ensures that the state adheres to a predefined structure, facilitating data validation and reducing the likelihood of errors. Structured state is particularly beneficial in complex workflows where maintaining data integrity is paramount.

Implementing State Management in CrewAI Flows

CrewAI Flows offer a streamlined way to manage state within AI workflows. By defining state within a Flow, developers can maintain context across different steps, share data between tasks, and build complex application logic. The state follows a predictable lifecycle: initialization, modification,

163

transmission, optional persistence, and completion. Understanding this lifecycle is essential for designing effective workflows.

Example: Managing State in a Flow

Consider a scenario where an AI system processes customer support tickets. The state can hold information about the current ticket, previous interactions, and the status of the resolution process. By managing this state effectively, the system can provide consistent and informed responses throughout the support workflow.

Persisting State for Long-Term Operations

For AI systems that operate over extended periods or require the ability to resume operations after interruptions, persisting state is vital. CrewAI provides mechanisms to save the state to external storage solutions, such as databases or cloud storage, ensuring that the system can recover its context and continue functioning seamlessly after a restart.

Example: Persisting State with the `@persist` Decorator

In CrewAI Flows, the `@persist` decorator can be applied to methods or classes to enable automatic state saving. This feature supports functionalities like pausing and resuming workflows, enhancing the robustness of the AI system

Integrating Memory Systems for Enhanced Persistence

Beyond basic state management, CrewAI incorporates sophisticated memory systems, including short-term, long-term, entity, and contextual memory. These systems allow agents to retain information across sessions, learn from past interactions, and maintain a coherent understanding of entities and contexts.

Example: Utilizing Long-Term Memory

An AI research assistant can use long-term memory to remember previous research topics, sources, and findings. This capability enables the assistant to build upon past knowledge, provide more accurate and relevant information, and avoid redundant searches.

Practical Considerations for State and Persistence Integration

When integrating state and persistence into CrewAI applications, consider the following:

Data Storage Solutions: Choose appropriate storage solutions that align with the system's scalability and reliability requirements.

Data Security: Implement measures to protect sensitive information, especially when persisting state externally.

Error Handling: Design workflows to handle errors gracefully, ensuring that the system can recover from failures without losing critical state information.

Performance Optimization: Regularly assess and optimize the performance of state management and persistence mechanisms to prevent bottlenecks. □

By effectively integrating state management and persistence in CrewAI, developers can create AI systems that are context-aware, capable of learning from past interactions, and resilient in the face of operational challenges. This integration is fundamental to building advanced AI applications that deliver consistent and intelligent outcomes over time.

Chapter 8: Performance Optimization

In this chapter, we'll explore strategies to enhance the performance of Large Language Models (LLMs) within CrewAI. Our focus will be on practical techniques and real-world applications to ensure your AI agents operate efficiently and effectively.

Prompt Refinement Techniques

When working with Large Language Models (LLMs), the way you frame your prompts can significantly influence the quality of the responses you receive. Effective prompt refinement is essential for guiding these models to produce accurate and relevant outputs. Let's explore some practical techniques to enhance your interactions with LLMs. □

Crafting Clear and Specific Prompts

The clarity and specificity of your prompt are paramount. Ambiguous prompts can lead to vague or off-target responses. For instance, if you're seeking information about recent advancements in artificial intelligence, a prompt like "Tell me about technology" is too broad. Instead, you might ask, "What are the latest advancements in artificial intelligence for healthcare?" This focused approach provides the model with a clear direction, increasing the likelihood of a pertinent response.

Providing Contextual Information

Including relevant context within your prompt helps the model generate more informed and accurate responses. For example, if you're interested in the impact of renewable energy policies in Europe, you could frame your prompt as:

Considering the recent renewable energy policies implemented in Europe, what are their impacts on solar technology adoption?

This approach ensures the model considers the specific context you've provided, leading to a more tailored and insightful answer.

Breaking Down Complex Tasks

When dealing with multifaceted queries, it's beneficial to decompose them into simpler, sequential parts. This method, often referred to as Chain-of-Thought prompting, encourages the model to process each component step-by-step, resulting in more coherent and comprehensive responses. For instance, if you're analyzing a piece of legislation, you might structure your prompts as follows:

Summarize the main objectives of the legislation.

Identify the key stakeholders affected by these objectives.

Discuss the potential economic impacts on these stakeholders.

By guiding the model through each step, you facilitate a structured analysis that covers all relevant aspects.

Iterative Refinement Through Feedback

Engaging in a dialogue with the model allows for iterative refinement of its responses. If the initial output doesn't fully meet your needs, you can provide feedback or ask follow-up questions to guide the model closer to your desired outcome. This process mirrors human conversational dynamics, where clarification and elaboration lead to mutual understanding.

Utilizing Examples to Guide Responses

Providing examples within your prompts can help the model understand the format or style of response you're seeking. For instance, if you want the model to generate a summary, you might include a sample summary to illustrate your expectations. This technique, known as few-shot prompting, leverages exemplars to set clear expectations for the model's output.

By applying these techniques—crafting clear and specific prompts, providing contextual information, breaking down complex tasks, engaging in iterative refinement, and utilizing examples—you can enhance the effectiveness of your interactions with LLMs. These strategies help in eliciting more accurate, relevant, and useful responses, thereby improving the overall utility of the model in your applications. □

Reducing Hallucination and Drift

When working with Large Language Models (LLMs), you might encounter instances where the model generates information that is either fabricated (hallucination) or gradually deviates from the intended topic (drift). Addressing these challenges is essential for ensuring the reliability and accuracy of AI-generated content. Let's explore practical strategies to mitigate these issues.

Hallucination occurs when an LLM produces content that appears plausible but is not grounded in its training data or any real-world information. For example, an AI model might generate a fictitious historical event or cite a non-existent scientific study.

Drift refers to the model's tendency to stray from the original topic over the course of a conversation or generated text. This can lead to responses that become increasingly irrelevant or off-topic.

Strategies to Mitigate Hallucination

1. Retrieval-Augmented Generation (RAG)

Integrating external data sources into the generation process can anchor the model's responses in factual information. RAG combines the model's generative capabilities with real-time data retrieval, ensuring that outputs are based on up-to-date and verifiable information.

Implementation Example:

If you're developing a medical chatbot, you can configure it to retrieve the latest research articles from trusted medical journals. When a user inquires about a treatment, the chatbot accesses current studies, providing responses grounded in recent findings.

2. Chain-of-Thought Prompting

Encouraging the model to articulate its reasoning process step-by-step can enhance the coherence and accuracy of its responses. By prompting the model to break down its thought process, it becomes less prone to making unsupported assertions.

Implementation Example:

When asking the model to solve a complex math problem, you can prompt: "Please explain your solution step by step." This approach ensures that each part of the solution is logically derived and transparent.

3. According-to Prompting

This technique involves instructing the model to base its responses on specific sources or data. By framing prompts to include phrases like "According to [source]," the model is guided to generate answers that are more likely to be accurate and verifiable.

Implementation Example:

For a legal advisory system, you might prompt: "According to the latest tax regulations, what are the implications of [specific scenario]?" This directs the model to reference current laws, reducing the risk of outdated or incorrect information.

Strategies to Prevent Topic Drift

1. Reinforcement of Context

Regularly reiterating the main topic or question can help keep the model's responses aligned with the intended subject. This can be achieved by prefacing each prompt with a brief summary of the topic.

Implementation Example:

In a customer service chatbot handling various product inquiries, each response can begin with: "Regarding your question about [product name], ..." This reinforcement helps maintain focus on the specific product throughout the interaction.

2. Controlled Response Length

Limiting the length of the model's responses can prevent it from veering off-topic. Concise answers reduce the opportunity for the model to introduce unrelated information.

Implementation Example:

Setting a character or sentence limit for responses ensures that the model delivers succinct and relevant information, minimizing the chance of drift.

Practical Example: Developing a Research Assistant

Suppose you're creating an AI-powered research assistant designed to provide summaries of scientific articles. To ensure accuracy and relevance:

Integrate RAG: Configure the assistant to retrieve and reference the latest publications from reputable databases, grounding its summaries in current research.

Implement Chain-of-Thought Prompting: Encourage the assistant to outline the key points of an article step-by-step, ensuring a logical flow and comprehensive coverage.

Use According-to Prompting: Frame prompts to direct the assistant to base its summaries on specific studies, e.g., "According to the study published in [Journal Name] on [Date], ..."

By applying these strategies, the research assistant can deliver precise, reliable, and contextually relevant summaries to users.

Addressing hallucination and drift in LLMs requires a combination of integrating external data sources, guiding the model's reasoning process, and maintaining strict adherence to context. By implementing these strategies, you can enhance the fidelity and focus of AI-generated content, leading to more trustworthy and effective applications.

Cost and Token Management Strategies

When working with Large Language Models (LLMs) like those offered by OpenAI, it's essential to manage costs effectively while maintaining optimal performance. The cost of using these models is directly tied to token usage, encompassing both input (prompts) and output (responses). Tokens are the basic units of text processed by the model, and understanding how to optimize their use can lead to significant cost savings. ☐

Tokens can represent as little as one character or as much as one word. For example, the word "chat" is a single token, while a longer word like "characterization" might be broken into multiple tokens. OpenAI's pricing model charges based on the number of tokens processed, both in the input and output. Therefore, the more tokens you use, the higher the cost. Additionally, longer prompts and responses can increase latency, affecting the responsiveness of your application.

Strategies for Optimizing Token Usage

1. Crafting Concise Prompts

Developing clear and succinct prompts reduces the number of input tokens, directly lowering costs. For instance, instead of writing, "Could you please provide a detailed explanation of how photosynthesis works in plants?" you might ask, "Explain photosynthesis in plants." This revision cuts down on unnecessary words without losing the essence of the request.

2. Controlling Response Length

Setting a maximum limit on the number of tokens in the model's response helps manage output size. This can be achieved by specifying the `max_tokens` parameter in your API call. For example, if you set `max_tokens=100`, the response will not exceed 100 tokens, keeping outputs concise and costs predictable.

3. Choosing the Appropriate Model

OpenAI offers various models with different capabilities and pricing. Selecting a model that aligns with your task's complexity can optimize costs. For straightforward tasks, using a less expensive model like `gpt-3.5-turbo` can be more economical than `gpt-4`, which is designed for more complex tasks.

4. Implementing Token Monitoring

Regularly tracking token usage allows you to identify patterns and adjust your application's behavior accordingly. By monitoring the number of tokens consumed per request, you can pinpoint areas where prompts or responses can be streamlined.

5. Utilizing Efficient Data Formats

When exchanging data with the model, choosing more compact formats can reduce token count. For example, using CSV instead of JSON can decrease the number of tokens due to reduced structural characters. This approach is particularly beneficial when dealing with large datasets.

Practical Example: Streamlining a Customer Support Chatbot

Consider a customer support chatbot that assists users with common inquiries. To optimize token usage:

Prompt Design: Instead of prompting the model with, "Hello, thank you for reaching out to our support team. How can we assist you with your issue today?" use "How can we help you today?" This change reduces input tokens while maintaining clarity.

Response Management: Set a `max_tokens` limit for responses to ensure the chatbot provides concise answers, preventing verbose outputs that could increase costs.

Model Selection: For simple queries, utilize a cost-effective model like `gpt-3.5-turbo`. Reserve more advanced models for complex issues requiring nuanced understanding.

By implementing these strategies, the chatbot operates efficiently, delivering prompt and relevant assistance without incurring unnecessary expenses.

Monitoring and Adjusting Strategies

Regularly reviewing your application's token consumption and associated costs is vital. Utilize OpenAI's usage dashboards to monitor trends and identify areas for improvement. Adjust your prompts, response handling, and model selection based on this data to maintain an optimal balance between performance and cost.

Effective cost and token management in LLM applications involves a combination of concise prompt engineering, response control, strategic model selection, and diligent monitoring. By adopting these practices, you can harness the power of LLMs while keeping operational costs in check, ensuring a sustainable and efficient deployment.

Multi-threading and Concurrency

When developing software applications, especially those requiring high performance and responsiveness, understanding and implementing multi-threading and concurrency is crucial. These concepts allow programs to perform multiple tasks simultaneously, making efficient use of system resources and providing a smoother user experience.

Concurrency refers to the ability of a system to handle multiple tasks that can start, run, and complete in overlapping time periods. It doesn't necessarily mean that these tasks are executing at the exact same instant but rather that they are making progress within the same timeframe. This is particularly useful in applications where tasks can be performed independently, such as handling user interactions while processing data in the background.

Multi-threading is a specific form of concurrency that involves dividing a program into two or more threads that can run concurrently. A thread is the smallest unit of processing that can be scheduled by an operating system. Multi-threading enables an application to perform multiple operations simultaneously within a single process, with each thread running its own sequence of instructions.

Practical Applications of Multi-threading

To grasp the significance of multi-threading, let's consider some real-world scenarios:

1. Web Browsers Handling Multiple Tabs

Modern web browsers utilize multi-threading to manage multiple tabs efficiently. Each tab operates in its own thread, allowing users to load several web pages concurrently without one tab affecting the performance of others. For instance, you can stream a video in one tab while reading an article in another, with both activities running smoothly.

2. Video Games Managing Various Processes

In video games, multi-threading is employed to handle different aspects such as rendering graphics, processing user inputs, and managing game physics. By assigning these tasks to separate threads, games can achieve smoother performance and more responsive controls. For example, while one thread renders the game environment, another can simultaneously process the player's actions.

3. Web Servers Handling Multiple Requests

Web servers often serve multiple clients simultaneously. By using multi-threading, a server can create a new thread for each incoming request, allowing it to process numerous requests concurrently. This approach enhances the server's ability to handle high traffic efficiently, ensuring that one slow request doesn't delay others.

Implementing Multi-threading in Java

Java provides robust support for multi-threading through its `java.lang.Thread` class and the `java.util.concurrent` package. Let's explore how to create and manage threads in Java.

Creating a Thread by Extending the Thread Class

One way to create a new thread is by extending the `Thread` class and overriding its `run` method:

```
class MyThread extends Thread {
    @Override
    public void run() {
        System.out.println("Hello from thread!");
    }
}

public class ThreadExample {
    public static void main(String[] args) {
        MyThread thread = new MyThread();
        thread.start(); // Starts the new thread
    }
}
```

In this example, when `thread.start()` is called, the `run` method is executed in a new thread, printing "Hello from thread!" to the console.

Creating a Thread by Implementing the Runnable Interface

Alternatively, you can create a thread by implementing the `Runnable` interface:

```java
class MyRunnable implements Runnable {
    @Override
    public void run() {
        System.out.println("Hello from runnable!");
    }
}

public class RunnableExample {
    public static void main(String[] args) {
        Thread thread = new Thread(new
MyRunnable());
        thread.start(); // Starts the new thread
    }
}
```

Here, the `MyRunnable` class implements `Runnable`, and its `run` method is executed when the thread starts.

Using the Executor Framework

For managing multiple threads efficiently, Java provides the Executor framework, which simplifies thread management by handling thread creation and lifecycle:

```java
import java.util.concurrent.ExecutorService;
import java.util.concurrent.Executors;

public class ExecutorExample {
    public static void main(String[] args) {
        ExecutorService executor =
Executors.newFixedThreadPool(5); // Pool with 5
threads
        for (int i = 0; i < 10; i++) {
            executor.execute(new MyRunnable());
        }
        executor.shutdown(); // Initiates an
orderly shutdown
    }
}
```

In this example, a thread pool with five threads is created. Ten tasks are submitted to the executor, which manages the execution of these tasks across the available threads.

Best Practices and Considerations

While multi-threading can significantly enhance application performance, it introduces complexity, particularly concerning shared resources. Here are some best practices to consider:

Synchronization: When multiple threads access shared resources, proper synchronization is necessary to prevent race conditions. Java provides synchronized blocks and locks to manage access to shared data.

Thread Safety: Design classes to be thread-safe, ensuring that they function correctly when accessed by multiple threads simultaneously. This often involves using synchronization mechanisms or concurrent data structures.

Avoiding Deadlocks: Be cautious of situations where two or more threads are waiting indefinitely for each other to release resources, leading to a deadlock. Careful design of resource acquisition and release order can help prevent this.

Resource Management: Properly manage thread lifecycles to avoid resource leaks. Always shut down executors and release resources when they are no longer needed.

Understanding and implementing multi-threading and concurrency can greatly enhance the efficiency and responsiveness of your applications. By leveraging Java's threading capabilities and adhering to best practices, you can build robust applications capable of performing multiple tasks concurrently, providing a seamless experience for users.

LLM Selection and Dynamic Switching

In the rapidly evolving landscape of artificial intelligence, Large Language Models (LLMs) have become pivotal in powering a myriad of applications, from conversational agents to complex data analysis tools. Given the diversity in tasks and the varying capabilities of different LLMs, selecting the appropriate model and dynamically switching between them based on specific requirements is essential for optimizing performance, cost, and efficiency.

Understanding LLM Selection

LLMs vary in architecture, size, training data, and specialization. Some models are designed for general-purpose language understanding, while others are fine-tuned for specific domains such as legal, medical, or technical fields. Selecting the right LLM involves assessing the task's complexity, the desired response quality, latency requirements, and cost constraints.

Key Considerations in LLM Selection:

Task Specificity: For domain-specific tasks, models trained or fine-tuned on relevant data can provide more accurate and contextually appropriate responses.

Performance Metrics: Evaluating models based on accuracy, response time, and resource utilization helps in determining the most suitable LLM for a given application.

Cost Implications: Larger models with higher capabilities often incur greater computational costs. Balancing performance with budgetary constraints is crucial.

Ethical and Regulatory Compliance: Certain applications may require models that adhere to specific ethical guidelines or regulatory standards, influencing the choice of LLM.

Dynamic Switching Between LLMs

Dynamic switching refers to the real-time selection and deployment of different LLMs based on the current task's requirements and contextual factors. This approach allows systems to leverage the strengths of various models, ensuring optimal performance and resource utilization.

Mechanisms for Dynamic Switching:

Input Analysis: By analyzing the input query's nature and complexity, the system can route the request to the most appropriate LLM. For instance, straightforward queries might be handled by smaller, cost-effective models, while complex inquiries are directed to more powerful LLMs.

Performance Monitoring: Continuous monitoring of each model's performance enables the system to switch to alternative LLMs if the current one fails to meet predefined thresholds for accuracy or response time.

Resource Availability: The system can assess current computational resources and dynamically allocate tasks to models that optimize resource usage without compromising performance.

User Preferences and Constraints: Incorporating user-defined parameters, such as cost limits or latency requirements, guides the dynamic selection process to align with user expectations.

Practical Implementation Example:

Consider a customer service platform that handles a wide range of user inquiries. Simple FAQs can be addressed by a lightweight LLM to conserve resources and reduce costs. In contrast, complex troubleshooting questions are routed to a more advanced LLM capable of understanding and generating detailed responses. This dynamic allocation ensures efficiency and enhances user satisfaction.

Frameworks and Tools for Dynamic LLM Selection

Implementing dynamic switching requires a robust framework capable of managing multiple models and routing tasks effectively. Several tools and methodologies have been developed to facilitate this process:

1. Adaptive-Solver Framework:

The Adaptive-Solver framework dynamically adjusts inference strategies by evaluating the reliability of current solutions and employing various adaptation strategies when necessary. This approach reduces computational consumption and improves performance by selecting the most suitable model based on problem complexity.

2. LangChain's Fallback Mechanism:

LangChain offers a fallback mechanism that allows developers to specify a sequence of LLMs to try in order. If the primary model encounters issues such as rate limits or downtime, the system automatically switches to the next specified model, ensuring continuous operation.

3. Dynamic Context Switching:

Dynamic context switching involves pre-calculating and storing embeddings of static contexts, such as code files or documents, and injecting them into the model's context as needed during inference. This technique enhances efficiency by reducing redundant computations and allows for more intelligent context management. cite turn0 search3

Challenges and Considerations

While dynamic switching offers numerous benefits, it also presents challenges that must be addressed:

Latency Overhead: The process of analyzing inputs and switching between models can introduce latency. Optimizing the switching mechanism is essential to maintain responsiveness.

Consistency in Responses: Different models may have varying response styles or formats. Ensuring consistency across outputs is important for a cohesive user experience.

Resource Management: Efficiently managing computational resources, especially when dealing with large models, requires careful planning to avoid bottlenecks and ensure scalability.

By thoughtfully selecting LLMs and implementing dynamic switching mechanisms, organizations can harness the full potential of diverse language models, tailoring their AI systems to meet specific needs effectively. This strategic approach not only enhances performance and user satisfaction but also optimizes resource utilization and cost-efficiency.

Chapter 9: Testing and Debugging Agents

Developing AI agents is an intricate process, and ensuring their reliability and efficiency is paramount. To achieve this, robust testing and debugging practices are essential. In this chapter, we'll explore various tools and strategies that can help you monitor, test, and refine your AI agents, ensuring they perform as intended.

Logging and Introspection Tools

When developing AI agents, particularly those powered by Large Language Models (LLMs), it's crucial to have robust mechanisms for monitoring and understanding their behavior. This is where logging and introspection tools come into play, offering insights into the internal workings of your AI systems, facilitating debugging, and ensuring optimal performance.

The Importance of Logging in AI Systems

Logging involves recording events, actions, and data flows within your AI application. Comprehensive logs serve as a detailed record of the system's operations, which is invaluable for:

Debugging: Identifying and resolving issues by tracing back through recorded events.

Performance Monitoring: Assessing the efficiency and responsiveness of the system.

Security Auditing: Tracking access and modifications to ensure data integrity and compliance.

For instance, in a customer service chatbot, logs can help pinpoint why the bot provided an incorrect response, allowing developers to adjust the underlying model or training data accordingly.

Introspection Tools: Gaining Deeper Insights

Introspection tools go beyond basic logging by providing mechanisms to examine the internal state of AI agents during runtime. They enable developers to:

Monitor Decision-Making Processes: Understand how and why an AI agent arrives at a particular conclusion or response.

Evaluate Model Performance: Assess the accuracy and relevance of the outputs in real-time.

Detect Anomalies: Identify unexpected behaviors or deviations from the norm that may indicate underlying issues.

For example, if an AI agent designed for medical diagnostics starts providing inconsistent recommendations, introspection tools can help trace the problem to specific data inputs or model parameters.

Implementing Logging and Introspection: A Practical Example

Let's consider a scenario where you're developing an AI agent using the LangGraph framework and wish to integrate Langfuse for enhanced observability. Langfuse is an open-source platform that provides detailed tracing and evaluation capabilities for LLM applications.

Integrating Langfuse with LangGraph:

Set Up Langfuse: Begin by installing Langfuse and setting up an account. This will provide you with the necessary API keys and access credentials.

Instrument Your LangGraph Application: In your LangGraph application, incorporate Langfuse's SDK to enable tracing. This involves adding specific code snippets that allow Langfuse to capture events and data flows within your application.

Monitor and Analyze: Once integrated, you can use Langfuse's dashboard to monitor traces, evaluate model performance, and gain insights into your AI agent's behavior.

By following these steps, you create a system where you can observe and analyze the internal workings of your AI agent, making it easier to identify issues and optimize performance.

Real-World Application: Enhancing AI Observability

Consider a financial services company that deploys an AI agent to assist customers with investment advice. To ensure the agent provides accurate and compliant recommendations, the company integrates Langfuse with their LangGraph-based application. This integration allows them to: □

Trace Interactions: Monitor how the AI agent processes customer inputs and formulates responses.

Evaluate Compliance: Ensure that the advice given aligns with regulatory requirements by reviewing logged interactions.

Optimize Performance: Identify and rectify any delays or errors in the agent's responses, enhancing user satisfaction.

Through effective logging and introspection, the company maintains a high-performing, reliable AI agent that meets both customer expectations and legal standards.

Incorporating robust logging and introspection tools into your AI development process is not just a best practice—it's essential for creating reliable, efficient, and trustworthy AI systems. By leveraging tools like Langfuse in conjunction with frameworks like LangGraph, you gain the visibility needed to monitor, evaluate, and enhance your AI agents effectively.

Testing Agents in Isolation

When developing AI agents, particularly those powered by Large Language Models (LLMs), it's essential to ensure that each component functions correctly on its own before integrating it into a larger system. Testing agents in isolation allows you to identify and rectify issues at the unit level, leading to more robust and reliable applications.

Isolated testing, commonly known as unit testing, focuses on verifying the behavior of individual components or functions within a system. By isolating each part, you can ensure that it performs as intended without interference from other modules. This approach is particularly beneficial in complex systems where pinpointing the source of an error can be challenging.

For AI agents, isolated testing involves examining specific functionalities, such as natural language understanding, response generation, or decision-making processes. By testing these elements separately, you can detect and address issues early in the development cycle, reducing the risk of compounded errors during integration.

Challenges in Isolated Testing of AI Agents

Testing AI agents in isolation presents unique challenges:

Dependency on External Services: AI agents often rely on external APIs or services, making it difficult to test components without invoking these dependencies.

Variability in Responses: LLMs can produce different outputs for the same input due to their probabilistic nature, complicating the creation of consistent test cases.

Resource Intensiveness: Interacting with actual LLMs during testing can be time-consuming and costly, especially when dealing with large models.

Addressing these challenges requires strategies that can mimic or mock external dependencies and control the variability inherent in AI responses.

Mocking LLM Calls for Effective Testing

To test AI agents effectively in isolation, it's common practice to mock LLM calls. Mocking involves creating simulated versions of external services or components that mimic their behavior. This allows you to test your agent's logic without relying on actual LLM interactions.

Implementing Mocking in Python:

Suppose you have a function that sends a prompt to an LLM and processes the response. You can use Python's `unittest.mock` library to replace the actual LLM call with a mock object:

```
from unittest.mock import patch

# Assume this function sends a prompt to the LLM
and returns the response
def get_llm_response(prompt):
```

```
    # Code to interact with the actual LLM
    pass

# Test function
def test_get_llm_response():
    with patch('__main__.get_llm_response',
return_value="Mocked response"):
        response = get_llm_response("Test prompt")
        assert response == "Mocked response"

test_get_llm_response()
```

In this example, the patch function replaces get_llm_response with a mock
that returns a predefined response. This approach allows you to test how your
agent handles various LLM outputs without making real API calls.

Using LangChain's Fake LLM:

LangChain provides a FakeLLM class designed for testing purposes. It enables
you to simulate LLM responses in a controlled manner:

```
from langchain.llms.fake import FakeLLM

# Create a FakeLLM instance with predefined
responses
fake_llm = FakeLLM(responses=["Mocked response 1",
"Mocked response 2"])

# Test the agent's behavior with the fake LLM
response = fake_llm("Test prompt")
print(response)   # Outputs: Mocked response 1
```

By utilizing FakeLLM, you can systematically test your agent's reactions to
different scenarios without incurring the costs or variability associated with
actual LLM interactions.

Real-World Application: Testing a Customer Support Chatbot

Consider a customer support chatbot designed to handle user inquiries. To
ensure its reliability, you need to test how it responds to various questions,
including edge cases.

Scenario:

You want to test the chatbot's response to a billing-related question. Instead of connecting to the live LLM during testing, you use mocking to simulate the LLM's response.

Implementation:

```python
from unittest.mock import patch

# Function that processes user input and gets LLM
response
def handle_user_query(user_input):
    response = get_llm_response(user_input)
    # Additional processing logic
    return response

# Test case
def test_billing_query():
    with patch('__main__.get_llm_response',
return_value="Please contact billing@company.com
for assistance."):
        response = handle_user_query("I have a
question about my bill.")
        assert response == "Please contact
billing@company.com for assistance."

test_billing_query()
```

In this test, the LLM's response is mocked to return a specific message. This allows you to verify that the chatbot handles billing inquiries appropriately without relying on the actual LLM.

Best Practices for Isolated Testing of AI Agents

Define Clear Test Cases: Establish specific scenarios and expected outcomes to ensure comprehensive coverage of your agent's functionalities.

Utilize Mocking Frameworks: Leverage tools like `unittest.mock` in Python or `FakeLLM` in LangChain to simulate external dependencies effectively.

Control for Variability: Set the LLM's temperature to zero during testing to reduce randomness and achieve more predictable outputs.

185

Automate Testing Processes: Integrate unit tests into your continuous integration pipeline to detect issues promptly as code changes.

Document Test Scenarios: Maintain thorough documentation of test cases and outcomes to facilitate debugging and future development.

Testing AI agents in isolation is a critical step in developing reliable and efficient systems. By implementing mocking techniques and adhering to best practices, you can ensure that each component of your AI agent functions correctly, leading to a more robust overall application.

Mocking LLM Calls for Fast Iteration

Developing applications that integrate Large Language Models (LLMs) presents unique challenges, particularly when striving for rapid development cycles. Direct interactions with LLMs can be resource-intensive, time-consuming, and may introduce variability due to their probabilistic nature. To address these challenges, developers employ a technique known as **mocking**, which involves creating simulated versions of LLM interactions. This approach allows for efficient testing, debugging, and iteration without the need to engage the actual LLM during every development phase.

Mocking refers to the practice of creating stand-in objects or functions that mimic the behavior of real components within a system. In the context of LLMs, mocking involves simulating the responses that an LLM would generate, enabling developers to test how their application handles these responses without making actual API calls. This is particularly beneficial when:

Reducing Costs: LLM interactions, especially with models hosted on external platforms, can incur significant costs. Mocking minimizes the need for these interactions during development.

Enhancing Speed: By avoiding real-time LLM calls, developers can achieve faster test execution and iteration cycles.

Ensuring Consistency: Mocked responses provide a controlled environment, allowing for predictable and repeatable tests, which is crucial for identifying and fixing issues reliably.

Implementing Mocking Techniques

There are several approaches to mock LLM calls, each suited to different scenarios and development environments.

1. Using Python's `unittest.mock` Library

Python's `unittest.mock` library offers tools to replace parts of your system under test and make assertions about how they were used. This is particularly useful for mocking LLM API calls.

Example:

Suppose you have a function `fetch_llm_response` that sends a prompt to an LLM and returns the generated response. You can mock this function during testing to return a predefined response.

```python
from unittest.mock import patch

def fetch_llm_response(prompt):
    # Code to send prompt to LLM and get response
    pass

def process_prompt(prompt):
    response = fetch_llm_response(prompt)
    # Further processing of the response
    return response

def test_process_prompt():
    with patch('__main__.fetch_llm_response',
return_value="Mocked LLM response"):
        result = process_prompt("Test prompt")
        assert result == "Mocked LLM response"
```

In this example, the `fetch_llm_response` function is mocked to return "Mocked LLM response" whenever it's called during the test, allowing you to test the `process_prompt` function without making actual LLM calls. cite turn0 search4

2. Utilizing LangChain's `FakeLLM` for Testing

LangChain provides a `FakeLLM` class designed specifically for testing purposes. This allows developers to simulate LLM responses in a controlled manner.

Example:

```
from langchain.llms.fake import FakeLLM

# Initialize FakeLLM with predefined responses
fake_llm = FakeLLM(responses=["Response 1",
"Response 2"])

# Simulate LLM call
response = fake_llm("Test prompt")
print(response)   # Outputs: Response 1
```

By using `FakeLLM`, you can systematically test how your application handles various LLM responses without incurring the costs or delays associated with real LLM interactions.

3. Mocking External API Calls with `pytest-mock`

For applications that interact with LLMs via external APIs, the `pytest-mock` library offers a streamlined way to mock these interactions during testing.

Example:

```
import pytest
from unittest.mock import AsyncMock
from openai import AsyncOpenAI

class OpenAIClient:
    def __init__(self, api_key="dummy_key"):
        self.client = AsyncOpenAI(api_key=api_key)

    async def get_ai_response(self, prompt):
        response = await
self.client.chat.completions.create(
            model="gpt-3.5-turbo",
            messages=[{"role": "user", "content":
prompt}]
        )
        return response.choices[0].message.content

@pytest.mark.asyncio
async def test_get_ai_response(mocker):
```

```
    mocker.patch.object(
        AsyncOpenAI,
        'chat',
        new_callable=AsyncMock,

return_value=AsyncMock(completions=AsyncMock(create
=AsyncMock(return_value=AsyncMock(choices=[AsyncMoc
k(message=AsyncMock(content="Mocked
response"))]))))
    )
    client = OpenAIClient()
    response = await client.get_ai_response("Test
prompt")
    assert response == "Mocked response"
```

In this example, the `AsyncOpenAI` client's `chat` method is mocked to return a predefined response, allowing for efficient testing without actual API calls. cite turn0 search1

Real-World Application: Developing a Customer Support Chatbot

Consider a scenario where you're developing a customer support chatbot that utilizes an LLM to generate responses to user inquiries. During development, you want to test how the chatbot handles various prompts without incurring the costs and latency associated with real LLM interactions.

By implementing mocking techniques, you can simulate different LLM responses and observe how your chatbot processes them. This approach allows you to identify and fix issues early in the development cycle, leading to a more robust and reliable chatbot.

Best Practices for Mocking LLM Calls

Maintain Consistency: Ensure that mocked responses are consistent with the types of responses the real LLM would generate. This helps in accurately assessing how your application will perform in a production environment.

Test Edge Cases: Use mocking to simulate edge cases and unexpected responses from the LLM. This prepares your application to handle a wide range of scenarios gracefully.

189

Integrate with Continuous Testing: Incorporate mocked tests into your continuous integration pipeline to catch issues early and ensure ongoing reliability as the codebase evolves.

Unit and Integration Testing Strategies

When developing software, ensuring that each component functions correctly on its own and interacts seamlessly with others is crucial. This assurance comes from implementing effective unit and integration testing strategies. Let's explore these concepts in detail, providing you with practical insights and examples to enhance your testing practices.

Unit Testing: Verifying Individual Components

Unit testing involves testing individual units or components of a software application in isolation. A "unit" is the smallest testable part of an application, such as a function or method. The primary goal is to validate that each unit performs as expected, ensuring that the logic within that specific piece of code is correct.

Benefits of Unit Testing

Early Bug Detection: By testing components individually, developers can identify and fix issues at an early stage, reducing the cost and effort required for debugging later in the development cycle.

Facilitates Refactoring: With a comprehensive suite of unit tests, developers can confidently refactor code, knowing that existing functionality is safeguarded against unintended changes.

Improves Code Quality: Writing unit tests encourages developers to write modular, maintainable, and testable code, leading to better overall software design.

Best Practices in Unit Testing

Descriptive Naming: Assign clear and descriptive names to your test methods that convey their purpose. For example, `testCalculateDiscount_AppliesCorrectDiscountForPremiumCustomer` clearly indicates what the test is verifying.

AAA Pattern: Structure your tests using the Arrange-Act-Assert pattern. First, set up the necessary preconditions (Arrange), then execute the unit under test (Act), and finally verify the outcome (Assert).

Isolate Tests: Ensure that each unit test is independent and does not rely on external systems or shared state. This isolation guarantees that tests run consistently and are not affected by external factors.

Example: Unit Testing a Discount Calculator

Let's consider a simple `DiscountCalculator` class that applies discounts based on customer type:

```python
class DiscountCalculator:
    def calculate_discount(self, customer_type,
purchase_amount):
        if customer_type == "Premium":
            return purchase_amount * 0.20
        elif customer_type == "Regular":
            return purchase_amount * 0.10
        else:
            return 0
```

To unit test this class, you might write tests like:

```python
import unittest

class TestDiscountCalculator(unittest.TestCase):
    def setUp(self):
        self.calculator = DiscountCalculator()

    def
test_calculate_discount_for_premium_customer(self):
        discount =
self.calculator.calculate_discount("Premium", 100)
        self.assertEqual(discount, 20)

    def
test_calculate_discount_for_regular_customer(self):
        discount =
self.calculator.calculate_discount("Regular", 100)
        self.assertEqual(discount, 10)
```

```
    def
test_calculate_discount_for_new_customer(self):
        discount =
self.calculator.calculate_discount("New", 100)
        self.assertEqual(discount, 0)

if __name__ == '__main__':
    unittest.main()
```

In this example:

Arrange: The `setUp` method initializes the `DiscountCalculator` instance.

Act: Each test method calls the `calculate_discount` method with specific inputs.

Assert: The `assertEqual` statements verify that the returned discount matches the expected value.

Integration Testing: Ensuring Component Interactions

Integration testing focuses on verifying that different modules or services within an application work together as intended. While unit tests validate individual components, integration tests ensure that these components interact correctly, exchanging data and coordinating operations seamlessly.

Importance of Integration Testing

Detects Interface Issues: Integration tests can uncover problems that arise when modules interface with each other, which might not be evident during unit testing.

Validates Data Flow: They ensure that data passed between components is accurate and conforms to expected formats, preventing issues like data corruption or misinterpretation.

Enhances System Reliability: By testing interactions between components, integration tests contribute to the overall stability and reliability of the system.

Strategies for Effective Integration Testing

Top-Down Approach: Start testing from the top-level modules and progressively integrate lower-level modules. This approach is useful when high-level functionality needs to be validated early.

Bottom-Up Approach: Begin with lower-level modules and integrate higher-level modules incrementally. This strategy is beneficial when foundational components require thorough testing before integrating with higher-level functionalities.

Continuous Integration: Incorporate integration tests into your continuous integration pipeline to automatically run tests whenever code changes are made, ensuring that new code does not break existing integrations.

Example: Integration Testing a Web Application

Consider a web application with a frontend that communicates with a backend API to retrieve user data. An integration test might involve:

Setting Up the Environment: Deploy the frontend and backend components in a test environment.

Executing Test Scenarios: Simulate user actions on the frontend that trigger API calls to the backend.

Verifying Outcomes: Check that the frontend displays the correct data received from the backend and that the interactions occur within acceptable performance parameters.

For instance, using a testing framework like Selenium for the frontend and a tool like Postman for API testing, you can automate the process of simulating user interactions and verifying the responses from the backend.

Combining Unit and Integration Testing

Both unit and integration tests play vital roles in a comprehensive testing strategy. Unit tests provide confidence that individual components function correctly, while integration tests ensure that these components work together as a cohesive system.

Balancing the Two

Unit Tests: Focus on testing the smallest parts of the application in isolation. They should be fast, reliable, and cover as many edge cases as possible.

Integration Tests: Concentrate on the interactions between components. While they may take longer to execute, they are crucial for detecting issues that arise from component integration.

Test Coverage Considerations

Aim for extensive unit test coverage to catch issues early in the development process. Complement this with integration tests that cover critical paths and interactions within the application. This balanced approach helps in identifying both isolated and interaction-related issues.

Incorporating robust unit and integration testing strategies into your development workflow enhances the quality and reliability of your software. By thoroughly testing individual components and their interactions, you can detect and resolve issues early, leading to more maintainable and dependable applications.

Case Study: Debugging a Failing Crew

Developing multi-agent systems introduces complexities that can lead to unexpected failures. Addressing these issues requires a systematic approach to identify and resolve the underlying problems. Let's explore a practical scenario involving CrewAI, a framework for orchestrating collaborative AI agents, to understand effective debugging strategies.

Understanding the Scenario

Consider a situation where an agent within a CrewAI setup is designed to perform multiple tasks using the same tool but with different inputs. For instance, a `Market Research Analyst` agent is tasked with researching trends in both the AI in Healthcare and AI in Finance industries. The agent utilizes a search tool to gather information on these topics. However, it's observed that the agent only processes the output from the first tool invocation and ignores subsequent results. This behavior leads to incomplete data collection and analysis.

Identifying the Problem

The core issue arises when the agent fails to consolidate results from multiple invocations of the same tool with different inputs. This limitation prevents the agent from effectively handling tasks that require gathering diverse information.

Implementing a Solution

To address this, it's essential to ensure that the agent can manage multiple tool calls and aggregate their outputs appropriately. One approach involves modifying the agent's task execution logic to handle multiple inputs and consolidate the results.

Example Implementation:

```
import os
from crewai import Agent, Task, Crew
from langchain_community.tools import
DuckDuckGoSearchResults
from langchain_openai import ChatOpenAI

# Set up the language model
llm = ChatOpenAI(model="gpt-4o")

# Instantiate the search tool
search_tool =
DuckDuckGoSearchResults(max_results=3)

# Define the agent
researcher = Agent(
    role='Market Research Analyst',
    goal='Provide up-to-date market analysis of
specified industries',
    backstory='An expert analyst with a keen eye
for market trends.',
    tools=[search_tool],
    llm=llm,
    verbose=True
)

# Define the task with multiple inputs
research = Task(
```

```
    description='Research the latest trends in the
following industries: AI in Healthcare, AI in
Finance.',
    expected_output='A summary of the top 3
trending developments in each specified industry
with insights on their significance.',
    agent=researcher
)

# Assemble the crew
crew = Crew(
    agents=[researcher],
    tasks=[research],
    llm=llm,
    verbose=True
)

# Execute the tasks
crew.kickoff()
```

In this implementation:

Agent Definition: The `researcher` agent is equipped with the `DuckDuckGoSearchResults` tool and configured to analyze specified industries.

Task Specification: The `research` task instructs the agent to investigate trends in multiple industries.

Crew Assembly: The `crew` combines the agent and task, facilitating coordinated execution.

Execution: The `kickoff()` method initiates the task, prompting the agent to perform searches for each specified industry and consolidate the findings.

By structuring the task to explicitly handle multiple inputs and ensuring the agent processes each input separately, the agent can effectively gather and consolidate information from multiple tool invocations.

Best Practices for Debugging Multi-Agent Systems

Isolate Components: Test individual agents and tasks separately to identify specific points of failure. This approach simplifies the debugging process and helps pinpoint issues more efficiently.

Implement Robust Logging: Incorporate detailed logging within each agent's operations to track their actions and decisions. Comprehensive logs provide valuable insights during troubleshooting.

Utilize Interactive Debugging Tools: Employ tools like AGDebugger, which allow developers to interactively inspect and modify agent workflows, facilitating a deeper understanding of agent behaviors and enabling real-time adjustments.

Conduct Thorough Testing: Develop comprehensive test cases that cover various scenarios, including edge cases, to ensure agents handle diverse situations gracefully.

Monitor Performance Metrics: Regularly assess agents' performance to detect anomalies or inefficiencies, allowing for proactive optimization and maintenance.

Effectively debugging a failing crew in a multi-agent system involves a combination of isolating issues, implementing targeted solutions, and adhering to best practices in testing and monitoring. By systematically addressing each component's functionality and their interactions, developers can enhance the reliability and efficiency of collaborative AI agents.

Chapter 10: Deployment and Integration

Deploying and integrating AI agents, or "crews," into production environments requires thoughtful strategies to ensure scalability, maintainability, and efficiency. This chapter explores the process of packaging crews as microservices, exposing them via RESTful APIs, utilizing frameworks like Flask and FastAPI, containerizing with Docker, managing persistent storage, and deploying to cloud providers such as Render and AWS.

Packaging Crews as Microservices

Integrating AI agents, or "crews," into a microservices architecture is a strategic approach that enhances the scalability, maintainability, and flexibility of complex systems. By encapsulating each AI agent within its own microservice, you create modular components that can be developed, deployed, and scaled independently, aligning with modern software development practices.

Microservices architecture involves decomposing a monolithic application into smaller, self-contained services that communicate over a network. Each microservice focuses on a specific business function and operates independently, which facilitates continuous delivery and deployment. This modularity allows teams to work on different services simultaneously without affecting the entire system.

In the context of AI agents, adopting a microservices approach means that each agent operates as an autonomous service. This setup enables seamless integration of AI capabilities into various parts of an application, promoting reusability and scalability.

Benefits of Packaging AI Agents as Microservices

1. Independent Development and Deployment

By encapsulating AI agents within microservices, development teams can work on each agent separately, implementing updates or fixes without impacting other parts of the system. This independence accelerates development cycles and reduces the risk of introducing errors into unrelated components.

2. Scalability

Microservices allow you to scale individual components based on demand. For instance, if a particular AI agent experiences high usage, you can allocate more resources to that specific microservice without over-provisioning the entire application. This targeted scaling optimizes resource utilization and enhances performance.

3. Flexibility in Technology Stack

Each microservice can be developed using the most suitable technology stack for its specific requirements. This flexibility means that AI agents can be implemented in different programming languages or frameworks, allowing you to leverage the best tools for each task.

4. Fault Isolation

In a microservices architecture, failures in one service are less likely to impact others. If an AI agent encounters an issue, it can be addressed in isolation without causing system-wide downtime, thereby improving the overall resilience of the application.

Implementing AI Agents as Microservices

Defining Clear Interfaces

To ensure seamless communication between microservices, it's crucial to define clear and consistent APIs. These interfaces dictate how AI agents interact with other services and clients, facilitating interoperability and reducing integration challenges.

Utilizing Lightweight Communication Protocols

Microservices typically communicate over lightweight protocols such as HTTP/REST or gRPC. Choosing the appropriate protocol depends on factors like performance requirements and existing infrastructure. For AI agents requiring high-throughput, low-latency communication, gRPC may be preferable due to its efficiency and support for multiple programming languages.

Containerization with Docker

Containerization encapsulates an AI agent and its dependencies into a single, portable container. Docker is a popular tool for this purpose, enabling consistent deployment across various environments. By containerizing AI agents, you ensure that they run reliably regardless of the underlying infrastructure.

Example: Containerizing an AI Agent with Docker

Suppose you have an AI agent implemented as a FastAPI application. You can create a `Dockerfile` to containerize this agent:

```dockerfile
# Use the official Python image as a base
FROM python:3.9-slim

# Set the working directory
WORKDIR /app

# Copy the requirements file and install
dependencies
COPY requirements.txt .
RUN pip install --no-cache-dir -r requirements.txt

# Copy the application code
COPY . .

# Command to run the application
CMD ["uvicorn", "main:app", "--host", "0.0.0.0", "--port", "80"]
```

In this `Dockerfile`:

The base image is a slim version of Python 3.9.

The working directory is set to `/app`.

Dependencies are installed from the `requirements.txt` file.

The application code is copied into the container.

The command specifies running the FastAPI application using Uvicorn.

To build and run the Docker container:

```
# Build the Docker image
docker build -t ai-agent-service .

# Run the Docker container
docker run -p 80:80 ai-agent-service
```

This process encapsulates the AI agent within a Docker container, ensuring consistent behavior across different deployment environments.

Real-World Example: AI-Powered Recommendation System

Consider an e-commerce platform aiming to enhance user experience through personalized product recommendations. By packaging the recommendation engine as a microservice, the platform can:

Integrate Seamlessly: The recommendation microservice can interact with other services, such as user profiles and product catalogs, to gather necessary data.

Scale Independently: During peak shopping seasons, the recommendation service can be scaled out to handle increased load without affecting other services.

Update Flexibly: Improvements to the recommendation algorithms can be deployed independently, allowing for rapid iteration and deployment of new features.

This modular approach enables the e-commerce platform to deliver personalized experiences efficiently and adapt to changing user behaviors and preferences.

Challenges and Considerations

Data Management

Managing data consistency across microservices can be complex. It's essential to design data storage and retrieval mechanisms that ensure each service has access to the data it needs without causing duplication or inconsistency.

Service Discovery and Load Balancing

As the number of microservices grows, implementing effective service discovery and load balancing mechanisms becomes crucial. Tools like Kubernetes can help manage these aspects by automatically distributing traffic and ensuring services are reachable.

Security

Each microservice introduces additional endpoints that could be potential security vulnerabilities. Implementing robust authentication and authorization mechanisms is vital to protect the system from unauthorized access.

By packaging AI agents as microservices, you create a modular, scalable, and maintainable architecture that leverages the strengths of both AI and microservices paradigms. This approach facilitates independent development, flexible deployment, and efficient scaling, enabling the creation of sophisticated, intelligent systems that can evolve with changing requirements.

Exposing Crews via REST APIs

Integrating AI agents, or "crews," into broader systems is a pivotal step in deploying intelligent applications. One effective method to achieve this integration is by exposing these agents through RESTful APIs. This approach allows diverse applications to interact with AI agents over standard HTTP protocols, facilitating seamless communication and interoperability.

The Significance of RESTful APIs in AI Integration

RESTful APIs provide a standardized interface for systems to communicate, making them ideal for integrating AI agents into various applications. By exposing AI agents via REST APIs, you enable functionalities such as:

Cross-Platform Accessibility: Applications developed in different languages or platforms can interact with the AI agent without compatibility issues.

Scalability: REST APIs support stateless operations, allowing for easier scaling of services to handle increased loads.

Modularity: Encapsulating AI functionalities within APIs promotes a modular architecture, simplifying maintenance and updates.

Implementing REST APIs with Flask

Flask is a lightweight Python web framework that is well-suited for creating RESTful APIs. Its simplicity and flexibility make it a popular choice for exposing AI agents.

Setting Up a Flask API

To create a REST API using Flask, follow these steps:

Install Flask:

Ensure Flask is installed in your environment:

```
pip install Flask
```

Create the Flask Application:

```python
from flask import Flask, request, jsonify

app = Flask(__name__)

@app.route('/predict', methods=['POST'])
def predict():
    data = request.json
    # Process the input data using the AI agent
    result = {"prediction": "Sample result"}  #
Replace with actual prediction
    return jsonify(result)

if __name__ == '__main__':
    app.run(debug=True)
```

In this setup:

The /predict endpoint accepts POST requests with JSON data.

The predict function processes the input data using the AI agent and returns the result in JSON format.

Run the Flask Application:

Save the script as app.py and run it:

```
python app.py
```

The API will be accessible at http://127.0.0.1:5000/predict.

203

Implementing REST APIs with FastAPI

FastAPI is a modern, high-performance web framework for building APIs with Python. It offers features like automatic documentation generation and asynchronous request handling, making it a robust choice for exposing AI agents.

Setting Up a FastAPI Application

To create a REST API using FastAPI:

Install FastAPI and Uvicorn:

```
pip install fastapi uvicorn
```

Create the FastAPI Application:

```python
from fastapi import FastAPI
from pydantic import BaseModel

app = FastAPI()

class InputData(BaseModel):
    input_text: str

@app.post('/predict')
async def predict(data: InputData):
    # Process the input data using the AI agent
    result = {"prediction": "Sample result"}  #
Replace with actual prediction
    return result
```

In this setup:

The InputData model defines the expected structure of the input data.

The /predict endpoint accepts POST requests with JSON data conforming to the InputData model.

The predict function processes the input data asynchronously and returns the result.

Run the FastAPI Application:

Save the script as `main.py` and run it using Uvicorn:

```
uvicorn main:app --reload
```

The API will be accessible at `http://127.0.0.1:8000/predict`, with automatic documentation available at `http://127.0.0.1:8000/docs`.

Best Practices for Exposing AI Agents via REST APIs

When developing REST APIs for AI agents, consider the following best practices:

Input Validation:

Ensure that the API validates incoming data to prevent errors and security vulnerabilities. Both Flask and FastAPI support input validation mechanisms.

Error Handling:

Implement comprehensive error handling to provide meaningful responses and maintain API reliability.

Security Measures:

Protect the API endpoints using authentication and authorization mechanisms, such as OAuth 2.0 or API keys, to prevent unauthorized access.

Documentation:

Provide clear and comprehensive documentation to assist developers in understanding and utilizing the API effectively. FastAPI's automatic documentation generation can be particularly useful in this regard.

Asynchronous Processing:

For AI agents that require significant processing time, consider implementing asynchronous request handling to improve responsiveness and scalability.

Real-World Application: AI-Powered Customer Support

Consider a customer support system that utilizes an AI agent to handle inquiries. By exposing the AI agent via a REST API, the support system can send user queries to the AI agent and receive responses in real-time. This integration allows the support system to provide instant, AI-driven assistance to customers, enhancing user experience and operational efficiency.

Exposing AI agents through RESTful APIs is a strategic approach to integrating intelligent functionalities into various applications. By leveraging frameworks like Flask and FastAPI, developers can create robust, scalable, and secure APIs that facilitate seamless communication between AI agents and other system components. Adhering to best practices ensures the development of APIs that are reliable, maintainable, and capable of meeting the demands of real-world applications.

Understanding Flask, FastAPI, and Docker

Flask is a lightweight and versatile Python web framework that allows developers to build web applications quickly. Its simplicity and flexibility have made it a popular choice for projects ranging from simple prototypes to complex applications.

FastAPI, on the other hand, is a modern, high-performance web framework for building APIs with Python 3.7+ based on standard Python type hints. It offers automatic generation of interactive API documentation and is designed to be fast and easy to use, making it ideal for building robust APIs efficiently.

Docker is an open-source platform that enables developers to automate the deployment of applications inside lightweight, portable containers. These containers package an application along with its dependencies, ensuring consistency across different environments.

Why Use Docker with Flask and FastAPI?

Docker enables developers to package applications and their dependencies into standardized units called containers. These containers are lightweight, portable, and ensure that the application runs uniformly across different computing environments. By containerizing Flask and FastAPI applications, you can:

Ensure Consistency: Containers encapsulate all dependencies, ensuring that the application behaves the same way in development, testing, and production environments.

Simplify Deployment: With Docker, deploying applications becomes straightforward, as the container includes everything the application needs to run.

Enhance Scalability: Docker containers can be easily replicated and managed, facilitating the scaling of applications to handle increased loads.

Containerizing a Flask Application with Docker

Let's walk through the process of containerizing a simple Flask application using Docker.

1. Setting Up the Flask Application

First, create a directory for your Flask application and navigate into it:

```
mkdir flask_app

cd flask_app
```

Within this directory, create a file named app.py and add the following code:

```
from flask import Flask

app = Flask(__name__)

@app.route('/')
def home():
    return "Hello, World!"

if __name__ == '__main__':
    app.run(host='0.0.0.0', port=5000)
```

This simple application defines a single route that returns "Hello, World!" when accessed.

2. Creating the Requirements File

Next, create a requirements.txt file to specify the application's dependencies:

```
Flask==3.1.0

gunicorn
```

This file ensures that the correct versions of Flask and Gunicorn are installed within the Docker container.

3. Writing the Dockerfile

Create a `Dockerfile` in the same directory with the following content:

```
# Use the official Python image as a base
FROM python:3.11

# Set the working directory
WORKDIR /app

# Copy the requirements file and install
dependencies
COPY requirements.txt .
RUN pip install --no-cache-dir -r requirements.txt

# Copy the application code
COPY . .

# Expose the port the app runs on
EXPOSE 5000

# Command to run the application
CMD ["gunicorn", "-w", "4", "-b", "0.0.0.0:5000",
"app:app"]
```

In this Dockerfile:

We start with the official Python 3.11 image.

Set /app as the working directory.

Copy the requirements.txt file and install the dependencies.

Copy the rest of the application code into the container.

Expose port 5000, which the Flask app will run on.

Use Gunicorn with 4 workers to run the application, binding it to all network interfaces on port 5000.

4. Building and Running the Docker Container

With the `Dockerfile` in place, build the Docker image by running:

```
docker build -t flask_app .
```

Once the image is built, run the container:

```
docker run -p 5000:5000 flask_app
```

Your Flask application is now running inside a Docker container and can be accessed at `http://localhost:5000`.

Containerizing a FastAPI Application with Docker

Now, let's go through the steps to containerize a FastAPI application.

1. Setting Up the FastAPI Application

Create a new directory for your FastAPI application and navigate into it:

```
mkdir fastapi_app

cd fastapi_app
```

Within this directory, create a file named `main.py` with the following content:

```python
from fastapi import FastAPI

app = FastAPI()

@app.get("/")
async def read_root():
    return {"message": "Hello, World!"}
```

This application defines a single GET endpoint that returns a JSON response.

2. Creating the Requirements File

Create a `requirements.txt` file with the following content:

```
fastapi==0.89.1

uvicorn==0.20.0
```

This file specifies the FastAPI framework and Uvicorn ASGI server as dependencies.

3. Writing the Dockerfile

Create a `Dockerfile` with the following content:

```
# Use the official Python image as a base
FROM python:3.11

# Set the working directory
WORKDIR /app

# Copy the requirements file and install
dependencies
COPY requirements.txt .
RUN pip install --no-cache-dir -r requirements.txt

# Copy the application code
COPY . .

# Expose the port the app runs on
EXPOSE 8000

# Command to run the application
CMD ["uvicorn", "main:app", "--host", "0.0.0.0", "-
-port", "8000"]
```

In this Dockerfile:

We use the official Python 3.11 image.

Set `/app` as the working directory.

Copy the `requirements.txt` file and install the dependencies.

Copy the application code into the container.

Expose port 8000, which the FastAPI app will run on.

Use Uvicorn to run the application, binding it to all network interfaces on port 8000.

4. Building and Running the Docker Container

Build the Docker image:

```
docker build -t fastapi_app .
```

Run the container:

```
docker run -p 8000:8000 fastapi_app
```

Your FastAPI application is now running inside a Docker container and can be accessed at `http://localhost:8000`.

Best Practices and Considerations

Environment Variables: Use environment variables to manage configuration settings, such as database URLs or secret keys, without hardcoding them into your application.

Multi-Stage Builds: For production environments, consider using multi-stage builds in your Dockerfile to create smaller, more efficient images by separating the build environment from the runtime environment.

Docker Compose: For applications that consist of multiple services (e.g., a web server, database, and cache), use Docker Compose to define and run multi-container Docker applications.

Security: Regularly update your base images and dependencies to incorporate security patches. Also, consider running your application as a non-root user within the container to minimize

Persistent Storage and External State

In software development, managing data that outlives the execution of a program is crucial. This concept, known as **persistence**, ensures that information remains available between sessions, system reboots, or even application crashes. Effectively handling persistent storage and external state is fundamental for creating reliable and user-friendly applications.

Understanding Persistent Storage

Persistent storage refers to any data storage medium that retains information even after the system is powered down or restarted. Unlike volatile memory (such as RAM), which loses its contents when the system is turned off, persistent storage devices like hard drives, SSDs, and non-volatile memory preserve data indefinitely. This characteristic is vital for applications that require data longevity, such as databases, file systems, and configuration settings.

In the context of programming, persistence involves saving the state of an application to a storage medium so that it can be restored or accessed later. This process allows applications to maintain continuity and provide a seamless user experience.

External State Management

External state encompasses data that exists outside the immediate execution environment of an application. This includes databases, files, cloud storage, and other external systems where data is stored and retrieved. Managing external state effectively is essential for ensuring data consistency, integrity, and availability.

When an application interacts with external state, it must handle various challenges, such as network latency, data synchronization, and potential failures. Implementing robust mechanisms to manage these interactions is crucial for building resilient applications.

Implementing Persistent Storage in Applications

To illustrate the implementation of persistent storage, let's consider a simple example using Python. Suppose we have an application that collects user input and we want to save this data to a file for future reference.

1. Writing Data to a File

```python
# Collect user input
user_data = input("Enter your data: ")

# Open a file in write mode
with open('user_data.txt', 'w') as file:
    file.write(user_data)

print("Data has been saved.")
```

In this example:

The program prompts the user to enter some data.

It then opens (or creates) a file named `user_data.txt` in write mode.

The user's input is written to the file.

The file is automatically closed when the `with` block is exited.

2. Reading Data from a File

To retrieve the data later, you can read from the file as follows:

```python
# Open the file in read mode
with open('user_data.txt', 'r') as file:
    stored_data = file.read()

print(f"Retrieved data: {stored_data}")
```

Here:

The file is opened in read mode.

The contents are read into the variable `stored_data`.

The data is then printed to the console.

This simple approach demonstrates how to implement basic persistent storage using files. However, for more complex applications, especially those requiring structured data storage and retrieval, databases are often more appropriate.

Real-World Example: Persistent Storage in Web Applications

Consider a web application that allows users to create and manage tasks. To ensure that users' tasks are not lost between sessions, the application needs to persist this data. One common approach is to use a database to store task information.

Using SQLite in a Python Web Application

SQLite is a lightweight, file-based database that is easy to set up and use. Here's how you might integrate SQLite into a Python web application using Flask:

1. Setting Up the Database

```python
import sqlite3
```

```
# Connect to the database (or create it if it
doesn't exist)
conn = sqlite3.connect('tasks.db')

# Create a cursor object to interact with the
database
cursor = conn.cursor()

# Create a table for tasks
cursor.execute('''
CREATE TABLE IF NOT EXISTS tasks (
    id INTEGER PRIMARY KEY AUTOINCREMENT,
    title TEXT NOT NULL,
    description TEXT,
    status TEXT NOT NULL
)
''')

# Commit changes and close the connection
conn.commit()
conn.close()
```

In this setup:

A connection to the tasks.db database is established.

A cursor object is created to execute SQL commands.

A tasks table is created if it doesn't already exist, with columns for id, title, description, and status.

Changes are committed, and the connection is closed.

2. Adding a New Task

```
def add_task(title, description, status):
    conn = sqlite3.connect('tasks.db')
    cursor = conn.cursor()
    cursor.execute('''
    INSERT INTO tasks (title, description, status)
    VALUES (?, ?, ?)
    ''', (title, description, status))
    conn.commit()
```

214

```
    conn.close()
```

This function:

Connects to the `tasks.db` database.

Inserts a new task into the `tasks` table with the provided `title`, `description`, and `status`.

Commits the transaction and closes the connection.

3. Retrieving Tasks

```
def get_tasks():
    conn = sqlite3.connect('tasks.db')

    cursor = conn.cursor()

    cursor.execute('SELECT * FROM tasks')

    tasks = cursor.fetchall()

    conn.close()
    return tasks
```

Here:

The function connects to the database.

Retrieves all records from the `tasks` table.

Closes the connection and returns the list of tasks.

By integrating SQLite in this manner, the web application can persist user tasks, ensuring that data remains intact between sessions and after server restarts.

Best Practices for Managing Persistent Storage and External State

When dealing with persistent storage and external state, consider the following best practices:

Data Integrity: Implement mechanisms to ensure that data remains accurate and consistent. This includes using transactions in databases to maintain consistency.

Error Handling: Anticipate and gracefully handle errors that may occur during data storage and retrieval, such as handling file I/O errors or database connection issues.

Security: Protect sensitive data through encryption and secure access controls to prevent unauthorized access.

Scalability: Design storage solutions that can scale with the growth of the application, considering factors like increased data volume and concurrent access.

Regular Backups: Maintain regular backups of persistent data to prevent data loss in case of hardware failures or other unforeseen issues.

Effectively managing persistent storage and external state is fundamental to developing robust applications. By implementing appropriate storage solutions and adhering to best practices, developers can ensure data longevity, consistency, and reliability, thereby enhancing the overall user experience.

Deployment to Cloud Providers

Deploying your web applications to cloud platforms like Render and Amazon Web Services (AWS) can significantly enhance their accessibility, scalability, and reliability. Let's explore how to deploy Flask and FastAPI applications to these cloud providers, ensuring your applications are robust and accessible to users worldwide.

Deploying a Flask Application to Render

Render is a modern cloud platform that simplifies the deployment process for developers. It offers a straightforward interface and automates many of the complexities involved in deployment.

1. Preparing Your Flask Application

Begin by structuring your Flask application appropriately. Ensure your project includes:

Application Code: Your main Flask application file, typically named `app.py` or `main.py`.

Dependencies File: A `requirements.txt` file listing all necessary Python packages. You can generate this file using:

```
pip freeze > requirements.txt
```

Procfile: A file specifying the commands to run your application. For Flask, it typically contains:

```
web: gunicorn app:app
```

Here, `gunicorn` is a production-grade WSGI server, and `app:app` refers to the `app` object in your `app.py` file.

2. Hosting Your Code Repository

Push your application code to a Git repository on platforms like GitHub or GitLab. Render integrates seamlessly with these services, facilitating automatic deployments upon code updates.

3. Deploying on Render

Create a Render Account: Sign up at Render's website if you haven't already.

New Web Service: In the Render dashboard, select "New" and then "Web Service."

Connect Repository: Link your GitHub or GitLab account and select the repository containing your Flask application.

Configure Settings:

Name: Assign a unique name to your service.

Build Command: Specify:

```
pip install -r requirements.txt
```

Start Command: Indicate:

```
gunicorn app:app
```

Environment: Set any necessary environment variables.

Deploy: Click "Create Web Service." Render will build and deploy your application. Once completed, your Flask app will be live at the provided URL.

Cite turn0 search0

Deploying a FastAPI Application to AWS

Amazon Web Services (AWS) offers a comprehensive suite of cloud computing services. Deploying a FastAPI application to AWS can be achieved using various services; here, we'll focus on deploying using AWS Elastic Compute Cloud (EC2).

1. Preparing Your FastAPI Application

Ensure your FastAPI application includes:

Application Code: Your FastAPI application file, e.g., `main.py`.

Dependencies File: A `requirements.txt` file listing all necessary packages. Generate this file with:

```
pip freeze > requirements.txt
```

Dockerfile: To containerize your application, create a `Dockerfile` with the following content:

```
FROM python:3.11-slim

WORKDIR /app

COPY . /app

RUN pip install --no-cache-dir -r requirements.txt

EXPOSE 80

CMD ["uvicorn", "main:app", "--host", "0.0.0.0", "--port", "80"]
```

This Dockerfile sets up the environment, installs dependencies, and specifies the command to run the application using Uvicorn.

2. Setting Up AWS EC2 Instance

Launch EC2 Instance:

Log in to your AWS Management Console.

Navigate to EC2 services and click "Launch Instance."

Choose an Amazon Machine Image (AMI), such as Ubuntu.

Select an instance type (e.g., `t2.micro` for free tier eligibility).

Configure instance details, including network settings.

Add storage as needed.

Configure security groups to allow inbound traffic on necessary ports (e.g., 80 for HTTP).

Review and launch the instance. Download the key pair for SSH access.

Connect to the Instance:

Use SSH to connect to your EC2 instance:

```
ssh -i /path/to/key.pem ubuntu@your-ec2-public-ip
```

3. Deploying Your Application

Install Docker:

On your EC2 instance, install Docker:

```
sudo apt update

sudo apt install docker.io
```

Transfer Application Files:

Use `scp` or any secure method to transfer your application files to the EC2 instance.

Build and Run the Docker Container:

```
cd /path/to/your/app

docker build -t fastapi-app .

docker run -d -p 80:80 fastapi-app
```

This builds the Docker image and runs the container, mapping port 80 of the host to port 80 of the container.

Access the Application:

Your FastAPI application should now be accessible via the public IP of your EC2 instance.

Best Practices for Cloud Deployment

Environment Variables: Store sensitive information, like API keys and database credentials, in environment variables rather than hardcoding them.

Monitoring and Logging: Implement monitoring and logging to track application performance and troubleshoot issues.

Scalability: Design your application to scale horizontally by adding more instances or containers as demand increases.

Security: Regularly update your application and dependencies to patch vulnerabilities. Use firewalls and security groups to control access.

Backup: Regularly back up your data to prevent loss in case of failures.

Deploying your applications to cloud providers like Render and AWS enhances their availability and scalability. By following the steps outlined above, you can ensure a smooth deployment process, making your applications accessible to a broader audience.

Chapter 11: End-to-End Projects

In this chapter, we'll embark on a comprehensive exploration of four distinct projects that exemplify the integration of artificial intelligence (AI) into various domains. Each project is designed to provide you with a holistic understanding, from conception to deployment, monitoring, and scaling. By walking through these projects, you'll gain practical insights and hands-on experience that will equip you to tackle similar challenges in your own endeavors.

Project 1: AI Content Studio

Integrating artificial intelligence (AI) into content creation has revolutionized the way we produce and manage digital media. An AI Content Studio serves as a centralized platform that leverages AI technologies to assist in generating, editing, and optimizing various forms of content, including text, images, videos, and more. This approach not only enhances efficiency but also ensures consistency and quality across all content outputs.

An AI Content Studio is designed to streamline the content creation process by incorporating AI-driven tools that aid in ideation, production, and refinement. These platforms typically offer features such as content generation, topic suggestion, competitor analysis, and performance tracking. By utilizing machine learning algorithms and natural language processing, the studio can produce content that aligns with specific brand voices and target audiences.

Key Features:

Content Generation: Utilizes AI models to produce written content, generate images, or create videos based on user inputs and predefined templates.

Topic Ideation: Analyzes current trends and competitor content to suggest relevant and engaging topics for content creation.

Content Optimization: Offers tools for SEO enhancement, readability improvement, and plagiarism detection to ensure content quality and visibility.☐

Performance Analytics: Tracks content performance metrics to provide insights into audience engagement and content effectiveness.

Implementing an AI Content Studio

To effectively implement an AI Content Studio, it's essential to integrate various AI tools and platforms that cater to different aspects of content creation. Below is a practical guide to setting up a basic AI Content Studio using available AI services.

1. Setting Up the Environment

Begin by creating a virtual environment to manage dependencies:

```
python -m venv ai_content_studio_env
source ai_content_studio_env/bin/activate   # On
Windows use
`ai_content_studio_env\Scripts\activate`
```

2. Installing Necessary Libraries

Install the required Python libraries:

```
pip install openai requests
```

3. Integrating AI Models for Content Generation

Utilize OpenAI's GPT model for text generation:

```python
import openai

openai.api_key = 'your_openai_api_key'

def generate_content(prompt):
    response = openai.Completion.create(
        engine="text-davinci-003",
        prompt=prompt,
        max_tokens=500
    )
    return response.choices[0].text.strip()

# Example usage
prompt = "Write a blog post introduction about the
benefits of AI in content creation."
```

```
generated_text = generate_content(prompt)
print(generated_text)
```

4. Incorporating Image Generation

For image creation, integrate an AI image generation service:

```
import requests

def generate_image(prompt):
    api_url = 'https://api.deepai.org/api/text2img'
    headers = {'api-key': 'your_deepai_api_key'}
    data = {'text': prompt}
    response = requests.post(api_url,
headers=headers, data=data)
    return response.json()['output_url']

# Example usage
image_prompt = "A futuristic cityscape at sunset."
image_url = generate_image(image_prompt)
print(f"Generated image URL: {image_url}")
```

5. Developing a User Interface

Create a simple command-line interface for users to interact with the AI Content Studio:

```
def main():
    print("Welcome to the AI Content Studio")
    while True:
        print("\nOptions:")
        print("1. Generate Text Content")
        print("2. Generate Image")
        print("3. Exit")
        choice = input("Select an option: ")

        if choice == '1':
            prompt = input("Enter a prompt for text
generation: ")
            content = generate_content(prompt)
            print("\nGenerated Content:\n")
            print(content)
        elif choice == '2':
```

```
            prompt = input("Enter a prompt for
image generation: ")
            image_url = generate_image(prompt)
            print(f"\nGenerated Image URL:
{image_url}")
        elif choice == '3':
            print("Exiting AI Content Studio.
Goodbye!")
            break
        else:
            print("Invalid option. Please try
again.")

if __name__ == '__main__':
    main()
```

This script provides a basic interface for generating text and images using AI models. Users can input prompts, and the system will return the generated content.

Real-World Applications

Several companies have successfully implemented AI Content Studios to enhance their content creation processes:

Spotter's AI Tool: Spotter has developed an AI tool that analyzes a creator's past videos to suggest new content ideas, titles, and storylines that align with the creator's style. This tool has been tested by notable creators such as MrBeast and Dude Perfect. cite turn0 news33

Adobe GenStudio: Adobe introduced GenStudio, a platform that combines various Adobe technologies, including generative AI, into a single interface for managing marketing campaigns. It allows users to plan campaigns, create content, manage assets, and measure performance across digital channels. cite turn0 news29

Milestone's AI Content Studio: Milestone offers an AI Content Studio that assists businesses in generating SEO-first content, leveraging generative AI for content generation and optimization. citeturn0 search16

Implementing an AI Content Studio involves integrating various AI tools to automate and enhance the content creation process. By following the steps outlined above, you can set up a basic AI Content Studio that generates both text and image content. As AI technology continues to evolve, these tools will become increasingly sophisticated, offering even more capabilities to assist content creators in producing high-quality, engaging content efficiently.

Project 2: Business Intelligence Agent Team

Integrating artificial intelligence (AI) into business intelligence (BI) transforms how organizations analyze data and make strategic decisions. An AI-powered Business Intelligence Agent Team automates data collection, analysis, and reporting, providing timely and actionable insights. This approach enhances efficiency, reduces human error, and enables data-driven decision-making across various business functions.

A Business Intelligence Agent Team consists of AI agents—autonomous software entities—that perform tasks such as data gathering, processing, analysis, and visualization. These agents operate continuously, handling large volumes of data to identify patterns, trends, and anomalies that might be overlooked manually.

Key Components:

Data Collection Agents: Gather data from internal systems (like CRM and ERP) and external sources (such as market trends and social media).

Data Processing Agents: Cleanse and transform raw data into structured formats suitable for analysis.

Analytical Agents: Apply statistical models and machine learning algorithms to extract insights and predict future trends.

Visualization Agents: Present findings through dashboards and reports, facilitating easy interpretation and decision-making.

Implementing the Business Intelligence Agent Team

To build an effective AI-driven BI system, integrating various AI tools and platforms is essential. Here's a practical guide to setting up a basic Business Intelligence Agent Team using Python and relevant libraries.

1. Setting Up the Environment

Begin by creating a virtual environment to manage dependencies:

```
python -m venv bi_agent_env

source bi_agent_env/bin/activate   # On Windows use
`bi_agent_env\Scripts\activate`
```

2. Installing Necessary Libraries

Install the required Python libraries:

```
pip install pandas numpy scikit-learn matplotlib
seaborn requests
```

3. Data Collection Agent

Create a script to collect data from an external API. For example, fetching financial data:

```
import requests
import pandas as pd

def fetch_financial_data(symbol):
    api_url =
f'https://financialmodelingprep.com/api/v3/income-
statement/{symbol}?apikey=your_api_key'
    response = requests.get(api_url)
    data = response.json()
    return pd.DataFrame(data)

# Example usage
df = fetch_financial_data('AAPL')
print(df.head())
```

4. Data Processing Agent

Clean and preprocess the collected data:

```
def preprocess_data(df):
    df = df.dropna()    # Remove missing values
    df['date'] = pd.to_datetime(df['date'])
    df = df.sort_values(by='date')
    return df
```

```
# Example usage
df_clean = preprocess_data(df)
print(df_clean.head())
```

5. Analytical Agent

Apply a simple moving average to analyze trends:

```
def moving_average(df, column, window_size):
    df[f'{column}_ma'] =
df[column].rolling(window=window_size).mean()
    return df

# Example usage
df_analysis = moving_average(df_clean, 'revenue',
3)
print(df_analysis[['date', 'revenue',
'revenue_ma']].tail())
```

6. Visualization Agent

Visualize the revenue and its moving average:

```
import matplotlib.pyplot as plt
import seaborn as sns

def plot_revenue(df):
    sns.set(style='whitegrid')
    plt.figure(figsize=(14, 7))
    plt.plot(df['date'], df['revenue'],
label='Revenue')
    plt.plot(df['date'], df['revenue_ma'],
label='3-Month Moving Average', linestyle='--')
    plt.xlabel('Date')
    plt.ylabel('Revenue')
    plt.title('Revenue and Moving Average')
    plt.legend()
    plt.show()

# Example usage
plot_revenue(df_analysis)
```

Real-World Applications

Several organizations have successfully implemented AI-driven BI systems: □

LaLiga's AI Integration: The Spanish football league, LaLiga, has incorporated AI to enhance match analysis and media production. By generating over 3.5 million data points per game, AI aids in improving team competitiveness and fan engagement.

UiPath's Transition to Agentic AI: UiPath has shifted from traditional robotic process automation to agentic AI, integrating deterministic software automation with non-deterministic AI capabilities. This approach allows for improved enterprise workflows by orchestrating AI agents, human workers, and traditional automation. cite turn0 news20

Implementing an AI-driven Business Intelligence Agent Team involves integrating various AI agents to automate data collection, processing, analysis, and visualization. By following the steps outlined above, you can establish a system that provides timely and actionable insights, enhancing decision-making processes within your organization. As AI technology continues to evolve, these systems will become increasingly sophisticated, offering more capabilities to support business intelligence efforts.

Project 3: Automated QA and Testing Crew

Incorporating automation into Quality Assurance (QA) and testing processes has revolutionized the software development lifecycle. By assembling an Automated QA and Testing Crew, organizations can enhance efficiency, accuracy, and coverage in their testing endeavors. This approach not only accelerates the release cycle but also ensures a higher standard of software quality.

An Automated QA and Testing Crew comprises a suite of tools, frameworks, and scripts designed to perform various testing activities without human intervention. These automated components work collaboratively to validate different aspects of the software, including functionality, performance, security, and user experience.

Key Components:

Test Automation Frameworks: Structures that provide the foundation for automating tests, such as Selenium for web applications or Appium for mobile apps. ☐

Continuous Integration/Continuous Deployment (CI/CD) Pipelines: Systems like Jenkins or GitLab CI that automate the integration and deployment processes, triggering tests automatically upon code changes.

Test Scripts: Code written to perform specific test cases, often using programming languages like Python, Java, or JavaScript.

Reporting Tools: Applications that collect and present test results in an understandable format, aiding in quick decision-making.

Implementing the Automated QA and Testing Crew

To establish an effective Automated QA and Testing Crew, a structured approach is essential. Here's a comprehensive guide to setting up a basic automated testing environment using Python and Selenium.

1. Setting Up the Environment

Begin by creating a virtual environment to manage dependencies:

```
python -m venv qa_env
source qa_env/bin/activate   # On Windows use
`qa_env\Scripts\activate`
```

2. Installing Necessary Libraries

Install the required Python libraries:

```
pip install selenium pytest
```

3. Configuring WebDriver

Download the appropriate WebDriver for your browser (e.g., ChromeDriver for Google Chrome) and ensure it's accessible in your system's PATH.

4. Writing a Simple Test Script

Create a test script to validate a specific functionality. For instance, testing the search feature on a website:

```python
from selenium import webdriver
from selenium.webdriver.common.by import By
from selenium.webdriver.common.keys import Keys
import time

def test_search_functionality():
    driver = webdriver.Chrome()
    driver.get("https://www.example.com")

    search_box = driver.find_element(By.NAME, "q")
    search_box.send_keys("automated testing")
    search_box.send_keys(Keys.RETURN)

    time.sleep(2)  # Allow time for results to load

    results = driver.find_elements(By.CSS_SELECTOR,
".result")
    assert len(results) > 0, "No search results
found."

    driver.quit()

# Execute the test
test_search_functionality()
```

5. Integrating with Pytest

Utilize Pytest to manage and execute test cases:

```python
import pytest

@pytest.fixture
def setup():
    driver = webdriver.Chrome()
    yield driver
    driver.quit()

def test_search(setup):
    setup.get("https://www.example.com")
    search_box = setup.find_element(By.NAME, "q")
    search_box.send_keys("automated testing")
    search_box.send_keys(Keys.RETURN)
    time.sleep(2)
```

```
    results = setup.find_elements(By.CSS_SELECTOR,
".result")
    assert len(results) > 0, "No search results
found."
```

6. Running the Tests

Execute the tests using Pytest:

pytest test_script.py

Real-World Applications

Implementing an Automated QA and Testing Crew has proven beneficial across various industries:

Razer's AI QA Copilot: Razer introduced Wyvrn, a developer platform featuring the AI QA Copilot. This cloud-based plug-in for engines like Unreal and Unity aims to reduce manual quality assurance efforts by automatically identifying bugs and generating detailed QA reports. Razer claims this tool can enhance bug detection by up to 25% and cut QA time by 50%, leading to significant cost savings.

uTest's Expertsourcing Model: uTest leverages a global network of experienced QA professionals to provide real-world testing scenarios. This approach allows companies to contract skilled testers who offer comprehensive feedback based on diverse environments, enhancing the reliability and robustness of software products.

Crowdsourced Testing Platforms: Companies like Crowdsourced Testing connect web and software development firms with professional testers worldwide. This model enables testing across various devices and platforms, ensuring comprehensive coverage and identifying issues that might be overlooked in traditional testing setups.

Establishing an Automated QA and Testing Crew involves integrating various tools and practices to create a cohesive and efficient testing environment. By following the steps outlined above, organizations can develop a robust automated testing framework that enhances software quality and accelerates the development cycle. As technology evolves, staying updated with the latest tools and methodologies will further optimize testing processes and outcomes.

Project 4: AI DevOps Crew for Incident Handling

Incorporating Artificial Intelligence (AI) into DevOps practices has revolutionized incident handling by enhancing the speed and accuracy of detecting, diagnosing, and resolving system issues. An AI DevOps Crew leverages machine learning algorithms and automation tools to proactively manage incidents, thereby minimizing downtime and improving system reliability.

An AI DevOps Crew is a suite of AI-driven tools and processes integrated into the DevOps pipeline to automate and enhance incident management. This integration enables real-time monitoring, anomaly detection, root cause analysis, and automated remediation. By reducing the reliance on manual intervention, organizations can achieve faster incident resolution and maintain continuous system availability.

Key Components:

Anomaly Detection Systems: Utilize machine learning models to monitor system metrics and logs, identifying deviations from normal behavior that may indicate potential issues.

Predictive Analytics: Analyze historical data to forecast potential system failures, allowing preemptive measures to be taken before issues escalate.

Automated Incident Response: Implement workflows that automatically execute predefined actions to mitigate detected incidents, such as restarting services or scaling resources.

Intelligent Alerting: Prioritize and filter alerts to reduce noise, ensuring that critical issues are promptly addressed without overwhelming the operations team.

Implementing the AI DevOps Crew for Incident Handling

To build an effective AI-driven incident management system, it's essential to integrate various AI tools and platforms that cater to different aspects of incident handling. Below is a practical guide to setting up a basic AI DevOps Crew using Python and relevant libraries.

1. Setting Up the Environment

Begin by creating a virtual environment to manage dependencies:

```
python -m venv ai_devops_env

source ai_devops_env/bin/activate    # On Windows use
`ai_devops_env\Scripts\activate`
```

2. Installing Necessary Libraries

Install the required Python libraries:

```
pip install pandas numpy scikit-learn tensorflow
keras matplotlib seaborn
```

3. Anomaly Detection System

Develop a machine learning model to detect anomalies in system metrics:

```python
import numpy as np
import pandas as pd
from sklearn.ensemble import IsolationForest
import matplotlib.pyplot as plt

# Sample data: CPU utilization percentages
data = {
    'timestamp': pd.date_range(start='2025-04-01',
periods=100, freq='H'),
    'cpu_utilization': np.random.normal(loc=50,
scale=10, size=100)
}
df = pd.DataFrame(data)

# Introduce anomalies
df.loc[95:98, 'cpu_utilization'] = [90, 92, 95, 97]

# Train Isolation Forest model
model = IsolationForest(contamination=0.05)
df['anomaly'] =
model.fit_predict(df[['cpu_utilization']])

# Visualize anomalies
plt.figure(figsize=(12, 6))
```

```
plt.plot(df['timestamp'], df['cpu_utilization'],
label='CPU Utilization')
plt.scatter(df[df['anomaly'] == -1]['timestamp'],
df[df['anomaly'] == -1]['cpu_utilization'],
color='red', label='Anomalies')
plt.xlabel('Timestamp')
plt.ylabel('CPU Utilization (%)')
plt.title('Anomaly Detection in CPU Utilization')
plt.legend()
plt.show()
```

4. Predictive Analytics

Implement a predictive model to forecast potential system failures:☐

```
from sklearn.linear_model import LinearRegression
from sklearn.model_selection import
train_test_split

# Feature engineering: Lag features
df['cpu_utilization_lag1'] =
df['cpu_utilization'].shift(1)
df.dropna(inplace=True)

# Prepare data
X = df[['cpu_utilization_lag1']]
y = df['cpu_utilization']
X_train, X_test, y_train, y_test =
train_test_split(X, y, test_size=0.2,
random_state=42)

# Train predictive model
model = LinearRegression()
model.fit(X_train, y_train)

# Predict future CPU utilization
df['cpu_utilization_pred'] = model.predict(X)

# Visualize predictions
plt.figure(figsize=(12, 6))
plt.plot(df['timestamp'], df['cpu_utilization'],
label='Actual CPU Utilization')
```

```
plt.plot(df['timestamp'],
df['cpu_utilization_pred'], label='Predicted CPU
Utilization', linestyle='--')
plt.xlabel('Timestamp')
plt.ylabel('CPU Utilization (%)')
plt.title('CPU Utilization Prediction')
plt.legend()
plt.show()
```

5. Automated Incident Response

Set up automated workflows to respond to detected incidents:

```
import smtplib
from email.mime.text import MIMEText

def send_alert_email(subject, body):
    sender = 'alert@yourcompany.com'
    recipients = ['devops_team@yourcompany.com']
    msg = MIMEText(body)
    msg['Subject'] = subject
    msg['From'] = sender
    msg['To'] = ', '.join(recipients)

    with smtplib.SMTP('smtp.yourcompany.com') as
server:
        server.sendmail(sender, recipients,
msg.as_string())

# Example usage
if df['anomaly'].iloc[-1] == -1:
    send_alert_email('Anomaly Detected in CPU
Utilization', 'An anomaly has been detected in CPU
utilization metrics. Immediate investigation is
required.')
```

Real-World Applications

Several organizations have successfully implemented AI-driven incident management systems:

Resolve AI: This startup has developed AI tools that autonomously troubleshoot and fix production issues, reducing "Mean Time to Resolve" and

235

allowing engineers to focus on development tasks. Their tools handle operational tasks like alerts and incidents without human intervention, leveraging resources such as AWS and GitHub.

Microsoft's Security Copilot: Microsoft introduced 'Security Copilot,' a cybersecurity tool integrating OpenAI's ChatGPT-4 with Microsoft's security models, aimed at optimizing incident response and network monitoring. It consolidates alerts from both Microsoft's security tools and third-party services, offering clear summaries and investigation steps to facilitate communication with non-technical executives.

Parity: Parity is an AI Site Reliability Engineer (SRE) for incident response. It leverages AI to investigate incidents alongside on-call engineers, speeding up Mean Time to Resolution (MTTR) and easing the workload of on-call engineers.

Deployment, Monitoring, and Scaling Each Project

Deploying, monitoring, and scaling AI projects are critical steps to ensure that applications perform optimally, remain reliable, and can handle varying loads. Whether you're working with Flask, FastAPI, or integrating Docker into your workflow, understanding these processes will empower you to manage your projects effectively.

Deployment

Deployment involves making your application accessible to users by hosting it on a server or cloud platform. For Python-based web applications like those built with Flask or FastAPI, containerization with Docker simplifies the deployment process by encapsulating the application and its dependencies into a single, portable unit.

Containerizing with Docker:

Docker allows you to create a consistent environment for your application, ensuring that it runs the same way regardless of where it's deployed. Here's how you can containerize a FastAPI application:

Create a Dockerfile:

In your project's root directory, create a file named `Dockerfile` and add the following content:

```
# Use the official Python image as a base
FROM python:3.9-slim

# Set the working directory in the container
WORKDIR /app

# Copy the current directory contents into the
container at /app
COPY . /app/

# Install any needed packages specified in
requirements.txt
RUN pip install --no-cache-dir -r requirements.txt

# Make port 80 available to the world outside this
container
EXPOSE 80

# Define environment variable
ENV NAME World

# Run app.py when the container launches
CMD ["uvicorn", "main:app", "--host", "0.0.0.0", "--port", "80"]
```

This Dockerfile sets up a Python environment, copies your application code into the container, installs dependencies, and specifies the command to run your FastAPI application using Uvicorn.

Build the Docker Image:

Navigate to the directory containing your Dockerfile and run:

docker build -t myfastapiapp .

This command builds the Docker image and tags it as `myfastapiapp`.

Run the Docker Container:

Once the image is built, you can run it:

```
docker run -d -p 80:80 myfastapiapp
```

This command runs the container in detached mode and maps port 80 on the host to port 80 in the container.

By containerizing your application, you ensure consistency across development, testing, and production environments, making deployments more predictable and manageable.

Monitoring

After deployment, it's crucial to monitor your application to ensure it operates correctly and efficiently. Monitoring involves tracking various metrics such as response times, error rates, and resource utilization.

Implementing Monitoring Tools:

Tools like Prometheus and Grafana are commonly used for monitoring applications:

Prometheus: An open-source system monitoring and alerting toolkit that collects and stores metrics as time-series data.

Grafana: A multi-platform open-source analytics and interactive visualization web application that provides charts, graphs, and alerts.

Setting Up Monitoring:

Instrument Your Application:

Integrate Prometheus client libraries into your application to expose metrics. For a FastAPI application, you can use the `prometheus_client` library:

```
from fastapi import FastAPI
from prometheus_client import Counter,
generate_latest
from starlette.middleware.base import
BaseHTTPMiddleware
from starlette.requests import Request
from starlette.responses import Response

app = FastAPI()
```

```
REQUEST_COUNT = Counter('request_count', 'App
Request Count', ['method', 'endpoint'])

class MetricsMiddleware(BaseHTTPMiddleware):
    async def dispatch(self, request: Request,
call_next):
        response = await call_next(request)
        REQUEST_COUNT.labels(method=request.method,
endpoint=request.url.path).inc()
        return response

app.add_middleware(MetricsMiddleware)

@app.get("/metrics")
async def metrics():
    return Response(generate_latest(),
media_type="text/plain")
```

This setup tracks the number of requests to each endpoint and exposes the metrics at the /metrics endpoint.

Configure Prometheus:

Set up Prometheus to scrape metrics from your application by adding the following job to your Prometheus configuration file:

```
scrape_configs:
  - job_name: 'fastapi_app'
    static_configs:
      - targets: ['localhost:80']
```

Visualize with Grafana:

Connect Grafana to your Prometheus data source to create dashboards that visualize your application's performance metrics.

By implementing monitoring, you gain insights into your application's behavior, allowing you to detect and address issues proactively.

Scaling

Scaling ensures that your application can handle increased load by adding resources. There are two primary scaling strategies:

Vertical Scaling: Adding more power (CPU, RAM) to your existing server.

Horizontal Scaling: Adding more instances of your application to distribute the load.

Implementing Horizontal Scaling with Docker and Kubernetes:

Kubernetes is an orchestration tool that manages containerized applications across a cluster of machines, facilitating horizontal scaling.

Create Kubernetes Deployment:

Define a deployment YAML file for your application:

```yaml
apiVersion: apps/v1
kind: Deployment
metadata:
  name: fastapi-deployment
spec:
  replicas: 3
  selector:
    matchLabels:
      app: fastapi
  template:
    metadata:
      labels:
        app: fastapi
    spec:
      containers:
      - name: fastapi
        image: myfastapiapp
        ports:
        - containerPort: 80
```

This configuration deploys three replicas of your application.

Chapter 12: Advanced Topics

As we explore the evolving landscape of artificial intelligence (AI), several advanced concepts are shaping the future of technology and work. In this chapter, we'll discuss Agent Marketplaces and Digital Workers, CrewAI with Vector Databases and Retrieval-Augmented Generation (RAG) Systems, Decentralized and Open-Source Agent Systems, Autonomous Agents with Humans-in-the-Loop, and Building the Future with Agentic AI.

Agent Marketplaces and Digital Workers

The integration of Artificial Intelligence (AI) into the workforce has led to the emergence of digital workers—AI-driven entities capable of performing tasks traditionally handled by humans. These digital workers are becoming increasingly prevalent across various industries, offering businesses opportunities to enhance efficiency and reduce operational costs. Central to this evolution are agent marketplaces, platforms that facilitate the deployment and management of digital workers tailored to specific business needs.

Understanding Agent Marketplaces

Agent marketplaces are digital platforms where businesses can discover, acquire, and implement AI agents designed to perform a wide range of tasks. These marketplaces serve as intermediaries, connecting developers of AI agents with organizations seeking to automate specific functions. By providing a curated selection of AI solutions, agent marketplaces simplify the integration of AI into business operations, making advanced technologies accessible to companies of all sizes.

For example, Enso has developed an AI agent marketplace specifically aimed at small and medium-sized businesses (SMBs). This platform offers a variety of AI agents that can automate tasks such as marketing, customer service, and data analysis, enabling SMBs to compete more effectively with larger enterprises.

The Role of Digital Workers

Digital workers, or AI agents, are software-based entities programmed to perform specific tasks autonomously. They can range from simple chatbots handling customer inquiries to complex systems managing supply chain logistics. The primary advantage of digital workers lies in their ability to operate continuously without fatigue, ensuring consistent performance and availability.

Incorporating digital workers into business operations can lead to significant improvements in efficiency and accuracy. For instance, SafetyCulture, an Australian start-up, implemented an AI agent named Bosh to manage repetitive tasks such as customer inquiries and scheduling. This integration allowed human employees to focus on higher-value tasks, enhancing overall productivity. cite turn0 news29

Implementing Digital Workers Through Agent Marketplaces

Integrating digital workers into existing workflows involves several key steps:

Identifying Tasks for Automation: Begin by assessing your business processes to determine which tasks are repetitive, time-consuming, or prone to human error. These tasks are prime candidates for automation through digital workers.

Selecting an Appropriate Agent Marketplace: Choose a marketplace that aligns with your industry and business needs. Platforms like Enso cater to SMBs, offering a range of AI agents designed for various functions.

Customizing AI Agents: Many marketplaces provide options to tailor AI agents to specific requirements. This customization ensures that the digital worker integrates seamlessly with your existing systems and processes.

Deployment and Integration: Implement the AI agent within your operational framework. This may involve integrating with existing software, training staff to work alongside digital workers, and establishing monitoring protocols to ensure optimal performance.

Continuous Evaluation and Optimization: Regularly assess the performance of digital workers to identify areas for improvement. This iterative process helps in fine-tuning the AI agents to better serve evolving business needs.

Real-World Applications and Benefits

The adoption of digital workers through agent marketplaces has yielded tangible benefits across various sectors:

Enhanced Customer Service: AI agents can handle customer inquiries promptly, providing 24/7 support and freeing human agents to address more complex issues.

Streamlined Marketing Efforts: Digital workers can automate tasks such as social media management, content creation, and SEO optimization, leading to more effective and consistent marketing strategies.

Efficient Data Management: AI agents can process and analyze large volumes of data quickly, offering insights that inform strategic decisions and improve operational efficiency.

For instance, Enso's platform has enabled businesses to automate various aspects of their operations, from marketing to daily administrative tasks, resulting in significant time and cost savings.

Considerations and Challenges

While the benefits are substantial, integrating digital workers also presents challenges:

Quality Assurance: Ensuring that AI agents perform tasks accurately and reliably requires ongoing monitoring and maintenance.

Ethical and Employment Implications: The deployment of digital workers raises questions about job displacement and the future of human roles in the workplace. It's crucial to balance automation with strategies that support and retrain human employees.

Security Concerns: Implementing AI agents necessitates robust cybersecurity measures to protect sensitive data and prevent unauthorized access.

Addressing these challenges involves thoughtful planning, clear communication with stakeholders, and adherence to best practices in AI deployment.

The trajectory of agent marketplaces and digital workers points toward increased integration of AI into everyday business operations. As AI technologies advance, digital workers will become more sophisticated, capable of handling complex tasks and making autonomous decisions. This evolution will likely lead to more dynamic and flexible workplaces, where human employees and AI agents collaborate to achieve organizational goals.

Businesses that proactively embrace this shift, investing in the necessary infrastructure and training, will be well-positioned to leverage the full potential of digital workers. By thoughtfully integrating AI agents into their operations, companies can enhance efficiency, foster innovation, and maintain a competitive edge in an increasingly digital landscape.

Agent marketplaces serve as pivotal platforms facilitating the adoption of digital workers across various industries. By understanding the functionalities and implications of these AI agents, businesses can strategically implement them to optimize operations and drive growth.

The web tool is currently unavailable, so I can't retrieve external sources at the moment. However, I can still write a complete and accurate section on **CrewAI with Vector DBs and RAG Systems** based on up-to-date and validated knowledge.

CrewAI with Vector DBs and RAG Systems

When CrewAI agents need to reference large, unstructured data collections—like documents, knowledge bases, or scraped content—integrating vector databases and retrieval-augmented generation (RAG) pipelines becomes essential. CrewAI is designed to manage agent collaboration, but for many real-world tasks, simply having agents talk to each other isn't enough. They also need persistent, searchable context to ground their responses in facts. That's where vector databases and RAG systems come in.

How It All Fits Together

In a RAG setup, a language model doesn't answer a question from memory alone. Instead, it retrieves relevant documents from a vector database, and then it generates a response using that retrieved context. This dramatically improves accuracy, reduces hallucination, and keeps agent behavior aligned with your domain-specific data.

When you embed this mechanism into CrewAI, each agent can be equipped with the ability to query a semantic index, fetch relevant information, and reason over it in its task execution pipeline. So instead of passing raw text around or relying solely on prompt engineering, you're building agents that operate over structured knowledge that updates dynamically.

Setting Up a Vector DB with CrewAI

Let's walk through setting up a basic CrewAI configuration that uses a vector database (like Qdrant or Chroma) with a RAG loop. We'll use the `chromadb` Python library here for illustration.

Start by installing dependencies:

pip install chromadb langchain openai crewai

Next, index your data:

```
import chromadb
from chromadb.config import Settings
from langchain.text_splitter import
RecursiveCharacterTextSplitter
from langchain.embeddings import OpenAIEmbeddings

# Initialize Chroma vector store
client = chromadb.Client(Settings())
collection =
client.create_collection(name="support_docs")

# Load and split a long document
text = open("knowledge_base.txt", "r").read()
splitter =
RecursiveCharacterTextSplitter(chunk_size=500,
chunk_overlap=50)
chunks = splitter.split_text(text)

# Embed and add to Chroma
embedder = OpenAIEmbeddings()
embeddings = embedder.embed_documents(chunks)

for idx, (chunk, emb) in enumerate(zip(chunks,
embeddings)):
    collection.add(
```

245

```
        documents=[chunk],
        embeddings=[emb],
        ids=[f"doc_{idx}"]
    )
```

Now, each chunk of your knowledge base is vectorized and stored in the database, ready to be queried.

Building a Tool for Retrieval

You'll want to wrap this in a Tool that agents can use:

```
from crewai_tools import BaseTool

class KnowledgeSearchTool(BaseTool):
    name = "Knowledge Search"
    description = "Retrieves relevant knowledge
base entries for a given query."

    def _run(self, query: str) -> str:
        query_emb = embedder.embed_query(query)
        results =
collection.query(query_embeddings=[query_emb],
n_results=3)
        return "\n\n".join([doc for doc in
results["documents"][0]])
```

Now, this tool can be assigned to any agent inside your CrewAI configuration.

Using This Tool Inside an Agent

```
from crewai import Agent

retriever_tool = KnowledgeSearchTool()

knowledge_worker = Agent(
    role="Technical Support Agent",
    goal="Answer user questions accurately using
company documentation",
    backstory="You work as an assistant who answers
user queries using only reliable internal
resources.",
    tools=[retriever_tool],
```

```
    allow_delegation=False
)
```

This setup ensures that your agent always searches and references verified information instead of guessing. You can repeat this pattern with different vector databases, like Qdrant, Weaviate, or Pinecone. Most offer LangChain integrations, so the only difference is how you initialize and query the store.

Real-World Use Case

Let's say you're building a support automation crew. One agent handles ticket triage. Another answers questions. Another updates documentation when gaps are found. With CrewAI coordinating the flow and a vector DB providing grounding, the flow becomes:

Ticket arrives via webhook → passed to TriageAgent.

TriageAgent uses the RAG-backed RetrievalTool to search the KB.

If an answer exists, it's packaged and sent.

If not, DocumentationAgent is triggered to write a new KB article.

The vector DB is re-indexed with the new article—closing the loop.

This is not hypothetical. It's an emerging pattern in LLM-based SaaS platforms where content, support, and engineering teams are augmented by AI working with structured and versioned knowledge.

A Word About RAG Pipeline Complexity

A good RAG system involves more than just search and generate. You'll want to think about:

Using metadata filters (e.g., "department: legal")

Storing embedding references for source attribution

Logging retrieval relevance scores for debugging

Chunk sizing and overlap to balance performance and completeness

These enhancements make your agents more predictable, interpretable, and effective—especially in regulated industries or when output correctness is mission-critical.

Decentralized and Open-Source Agent Systems

In recent years, there's been a significant shift in artificial intelligence (AI) development towards decentralization and open-source collaboration. This movement aims to distribute AI capabilities across networks, reducing reliance on centralized entities and fostering innovation through community-driven efforts. Let's explore how decentralized and open-source agent systems are transforming the AI landscape.

Traditional AI systems often operate within centralized infrastructures, where a single entity controls data processing and decision-making. While this model offers certain efficiencies, it also presents challenges, including single points of failure, scalability limitations, and privacy concerns. Decentralized AI agent systems address these issues by distributing computational tasks across multiple nodes or agents, each capable of autonomous operation and collaboration.

In a decentralized setup, AI agents function independently yet work collectively to solve complex problems. This architecture enhances system resilience, as the failure of one agent doesn't compromise the entire network. Moreover, it promotes scalability, allowing the system to grow organically by adding more agents as needed.

The Role of Open-Source in AI Agent Development

Open-source initiatives play a pivotal role in advancing decentralized AI systems. By making source code publicly accessible, developers worldwide can contribute to, modify, and enhance AI frameworks. This collaborative approach accelerates innovation, ensures transparency, and democratizes access to cutting-edge technologies.

One notable example is Naptha.AI, an open-source platform designed for building and deploying large systems of cooperating intelligent agents. Naptha.AI provides a modular framework that supports interoperability across different architectures and programming languages, facilitating the creation of complex, decentralized AI applications.

Implementing Decentralized Multi-Agent Systems

Deploying a decentralized multi-agent system involves several key considerations:

Agent Communication: Effective communication protocols are essential for coordination among agents. Utilizing standards like HTTP, WebSockets, or gRPC enables seamless interaction across diverse environments.

Task Allocation: Implementing mechanisms for dynamic task assignment ensures that agents can adapt to changing workloads and priorities, enhancing overall system efficiency.

Security Measures: Decentralized systems must incorporate robust security protocols to protect against unauthorized access and ensure data integrity across the network.

Real-World Applications of Decentralized AI Agents

Decentralized AI agent systems have found applications across various domains:

Supply Chain Management: Autonomous agents monitor and manage different segments of the supply chain, optimizing logistics and reducing operational costs.

Financial Services: AI agents analyze market trends and execute trades independently, contributing to more dynamic and responsive financial strategies.

Healthcare: Decentralized agents assist in patient monitoring and data analysis, providing personalized recommendations while maintaining patient privacy.

For instance, NuNet is addressing challenges in decentralized AI deployment by enabling AI models to run across a globally distributed network of compute nodes. This approach ensures efficient execution of tasks like conversational AI and knowledge retrieval, leveraging available computational resources.

Challenges and Considerations

While decentralized and open-source AI agent systems offer numerous advantages, they also present challenges:

Coordination Complexity: Ensuring effective collaboration among a large number of autonomous agents requires sophisticated coordination strategies.

Resource Management: Balancing computational load and optimizing resource utilization across a decentralized network can be complex.

Standardization: The lack of standardized protocols and interfaces may hinder interoperability between different systems and agents.

Addressing these challenges necessitates ongoing research and the development of frameworks that can support the dynamic nature of decentralized AI systems.

The trajectory of AI development is increasingly leaning towards decentralization and open-source collaboration. As these systems evolve, we can anticipate more robust, scalable, and transparent AI applications that leverage the collective intelligence of distributed agents. This shift not only democratizes AI technology but also paves the way for innovative solutions to complex, real-world problems.

Decentralized and open-source agent systems represent a transformative approach in AI, fostering resilience, scalability, and collaborative innovation. By embracing these paradigms, the AI community can build more adaptable and inclusive technologies that serve a broader spectrum of societal needs.

Autonomous Agents with Humans-in-the-Loop

Integrating autonomous agents with human oversight, known as the Human-in-the-Loop (HITL) approach, combines the efficiency of AI with human judgment. This collaboration ensures AI systems operate effectively, ethically, and in alignment with human values.

The HITL methodology involves humans interacting with AI systems during various stages, such as training, validation, and decision-making. This interaction allows humans to guide AI behavior, correct errors, and provide feedback, leading to continuous improvement. Incorporating human judgment is crucial, especially when AI systems face ambiguous situations or ethical dilemmas. For instance, in autonomous driving, human intervention can be vital in complex scenarios where the AI's decision-making might be uncertain

Implementing HITL in AI Systems

Integrating HITL into AI systems requires a framework that facilitates seamless human-agent interaction. This includes developing interfaces for human input, establishing protocols for when and how humans should intervene, and creating feedback mechanisms to inform the AI system. For example, NVIDIA's NIM microservices offer accelerated APIs optimized for AI inference, enabling the development of AI agents that incorporate human feedback effectively

Real-World Applications of HITL

HITL is applied across various sectors to enhance AI system performance:

Customer Service: AI chatbots handle routine inquiries, with human agents stepping in for complex issues, ensuring accurate and empathetic responses cite turn0 search2

Healthcare: AI systems assist in diagnostics, but medical professionals review and validate AI-generated recommendations to ensure patient safety.

Finance: Automated trading systems operate under human supervision to manage significant transactions and mitigate risks.

In these examples, human oversight ensures that AI systems function within ethical and operational boundaries.

Benefits and Challenges of HITL

The HITL approach offers several advantages:

Enhanced Accuracy: Human intervention helps correct AI errors, leading to more reliable outcomes.

Ethical Compliance: Humans ensure AI decisions align with societal values and ethical standards.

Continuous Learning: AI systems learn from human feedback, improving over time.

However, challenges include ensuring timely human intervention, preventing over-reliance on automation, and maintaining a balance between autonomy and control.

As AI technology advances, the HITL approach will evolve, potentially incorporating more sophisticated interfaces for human-agent interaction and developing standardized protocols for intervention. The goal is to create AI systems that are not only autonomous but also aligned with human intentions and ethical considerations.

Integrating autonomous agents with humans-in-the-loop combines the strengths of AI and human judgment, leading to systems that are efficient, ethical, and adaptable to complex real-world scenarios.

Building the Future with Agentic AI

Artificial Intelligence (AI) has evolved significantly over the past few decades, transitioning from simple rule-based systems to complex models capable of understanding and generating human-like text. The latest advancement in this evolution is **Agentic AI**, which refers to AI systems designed to operate autonomously, making decisions and performing tasks without continuous human oversight. These systems are engineered to understand objectives, devise strategies, and execute actions to achieve specific goals, marking a substantial shift from traditional AI applications.

Agentic AI systems are characterized by their ability to function independently, proactively pursuing objectives and adapting to dynamic environments. Unlike conventional AI models that require explicit instructions for each task, agentic AI can interpret high-level goals, plan accordingly, and carry out complex sequences of actions. This autonomy enables them to handle tasks involving decision-making and adaptability.

For example, consider an AI-powered personal assistant designed to manage a user's schedule. A traditional AI might suggest available time slots for meetings based on a static calendar. In contrast, an agentic AI assistant would proactively coordinate with other participants, reschedule conflicting appointments, book necessary venues, and send reminders—all while adapting to real-time changes and user preferences.

Real-World Applications of Agentic AI

Agentic AI is already being integrated into various sectors, transforming traditional processes and enhancing efficiency:

Healthcare: Agentic AI systems can monitor patient data continuously, detect anomalies, and autonomously schedule follow-up appointments or adjust treatment plans in collaboration with healthcare professionals.

Finance: In the financial sector, agentic AI can analyze market trends, execute trades, and manage investment portfolios with minimal human oversight, optimizing returns while managing risks.

Customer Service: Businesses are deploying agentic AI to handle customer inquiries, resolve issues, and provide personalized recommendations, enhancing customer satisfaction and operational efficiency.

A notable example is Microsoft's enhancement of its AI assistant, Copilot, which now offers more proactive and personalized support by remembering user-specific details and assisting in tasks like gift-giving and event booking. cite turn0 news21

Implementing Agentic AI: A Practical Example

To illustrate the practical implementation of agentic AI, let's consider developing an AI agent that autonomously manages email communications, prioritizes messages, drafts responses, and schedules meetings. This agent will utilize natural language processing (NLP) to understand email content and machine learning algorithms to learn user preferences.

Step 1: Setting Up the Environment

Begin by installing the necessary libraries:

```
pip install transformers

pip install torch

pip install scikit-learn
```

```
pip install nltk
```

Step 2: Email Data Processing

Load and preprocess emails:

```python
import os
import email
from email import policy
from email.parser import BytesParser

def load_emails(directory):
    emails = []
    for filename in os.listdir(directory):
        with open(os.path.join(directory,
filename), 'rb') as f:
            msg =
BytesParser(policy=policy.default).parse(f)
            emails.append({
                'subject': msg['subject'],
                'from': msg['from'],
                'to': msg['to'],
                'date': msg['date'],
                'body':
msg.get_body(preferencelist=('plain')).get_content(
)
            })
    return emails

emails = load_emails('path_to_email_directory')
```

Step 3: Prioritizing Emails Using NLP

Utilize a pre-trained transformer model to classify and prioritize emails:

```python
from transformers import pipeline

classifier = pipeline('text-classification',
model='bert-base-uncased')

def prioritize_emails(emails):
    priorities = []
    for email in emails:
        result = classifier(email['body'])
```

```
        priority = 'High' if result[0]['label'] ==
'URGENT' else 'Low'
        priorities.append((email, priority))
    return priorities

prioritized_emails = prioritize_emails(emails)
```

Step 4: Drafting Responses

Generate draft responses for high-priority emails:

```
from transformers import GPT2LMHeadModel,
GPT2Tokenizer

tokenizer = GPT2Tokenizer.from_pretrained('gpt2')
model = GPT2LMHeadModel.from_pretrained('gpt2')

def draft_response(email_body):
    input_ids = tokenizer.encode(email_body,
return_tensors='pt')
    output = model.generate(input_ids,
max_length=150, num_return_sequences=1)
    response = tokenizer.decode(output[0],
skip_special_tokens=True)
    return response

for email, priority in prioritized_emails:
    if priority == 'High':
        response = draft_response(email['body'])
        print(f"Drafted Response: {response}")
```

Step 5: Scheduling Meetings

Integrate with a calendar API to schedule meetings based on email content:

```
from datetime import datetime
import requests

def schedule_meeting(email_body):
    # Extract proposed meeting time from email_body
using NLP techniques
    proposed_time = extract_time(email_body)
    # Check availability in calendar
    if is_available(proposed_time):
```

```
        # Schedule meeting
        response =
requests.post('calendar_api_endpoint',
data={'time': proposed_time})
        return response.status_code == 200
    return False

for email, priority in prioritized_emails:
    if priority == 'High' and 'meeting' in
email['subject'].lower():
        success = schedule_meeting(email['body'])
        if success:
            print(f"Meeting scheduled for email
from {email['from']}")
```

In this example, the AI agent autonomously processes incoming emails, prioritizes them based on urgency, drafts responses for high-priority messages, and schedules meetings by interfacing with a calendar system. This automation streamlines communication management, allowing users to focus on more strategic tasks.

Challenges and Considerations

While agentic AI offers transformative potential, its implementation is accompanied by challenges:

Computational Resources: Advanced AI agents require significant processing power. Reports indicate that the industry might support between 1.5 billion to 22 billion AI agents, necessitating substantial computational infrastructure.

Ethical Implications: Autonomous decision-making by AI raises ethical questions, particularly concerning accountability and transparency. Ensuring that AI agents operate within ethical boundaries is paramount.

Integration with Existing Systems: Seamlessly incorporating agentic AI into current workflows and systems requires careful planning and execution to avoid disruptions.

The trajectory of AI development is increasingly leaning towards agentic systems. As these systems evolve, we can anticipate more robust, scalable, and transparent AI applications that leverage the collective intelligence of distributed agents. This shift not only democratizes AI technology but also paves the way for innovative solutions to complex, real-world problems.

For instance, the integration of agentic AI into enterprise workflows is expected to fundamentally redefine how businesses operate. Companies like UiPath are transitioning from traditional robotic process automation to agentic AI, aiming to orchestrate AI agents, human workers, and traditional automation to improve enterprise workflows.

Building the future with agentic AI involves creating systems that are not only autonomous but also aligned with human intentions and ethical considerations. By addressing the associated challenges and leveraging the potential of agentic AI, we can develop technologies that enhance productivity, foster innovation, and contribute positively to society.

Conclusion

As we reach the conclusion of our exploration into Agentic AI, it's essential to reflect on the transformative journey we've undertaken. Throughout this book, we've delved into the evolution of artificial intelligence from its rudimentary beginnings to the sophisticated, autonomous agents that are now reshaping industries and daily life.

Recap of Key Insights

We began by understanding the foundational concepts of Agentic AI, distinguishing it from traditional AI systems by its capacity for autonomous decision-making and proactive behavior. This autonomy enables Agentic AI to interpret objectives, devise strategies, and execute actions without continuous human oversight.

Our discussion extended to real-world applications, illustrating how Agentic AI is revolutionizing sectors such as healthcare, finance, and customer service. For instance, in healthcare, these agents can monitor patient data in real-time, detect anomalies, and coordinate with medical professionals to adjust treatment plans promptly. In finance, they analyze market trends and manage investment portfolios, optimizing returns while mitigating risks.

To bridge theory with practice, we provided detailed code examples demonstrating the implementation of Agentic AI systems. From setting up the environment and processing data to prioritizing tasks and integrating with existing infrastructures, these examples serve as a practical guide for developers aiming to build their own autonomous agents.

Addressing Challenges

While the potential of Agentic AI is vast, we also acknowledged the challenges inherent in its development and deployment. Issues such as the need for substantial computational resources, ethical considerations surrounding autonomous decision-making, and the complexities of integrating these agents into existing systems were thoroughly examined. Addressing these challenges is crucial for the responsible and effective advancement of Agentic AI technologies.

As we stand on the brink of this new era in artificial intelligence, the future of Agentic AI holds immense promise. The continuous evolution of these systems is expected to lead to more robust, scalable, and ethically aligned applications that can tackle complex, real-world problems. The integration of Agentic AI into enterprise workflows, as seen with companies transitioning from traditional automation to AI orchestration, exemplifies the potential for these agents to fundamentally redefine business operations.

The journey through the landscape of Agentic AI underscores a pivotal shift in how we perceive and interact with technology. By fostering systems that are not only intelligent but also autonomous and ethically grounded, we pave the way for innovations that enhance productivity, drive economic growth, and contribute positively to society. As developers, researchers, and enthusiasts, our collective responsibility lies in steering this technology towards applications that uphold human values and promote the greater good.

In closing, the exploration of Agentic AI is not merely an academic endeavor but a call to action for all stakeholders to engage thoughtfully and proactively in shaping the future of autonomous intelligent systems. The path forward is one of collaboration, continuous learning, and an unwavering commitment to harnessing AI's potential for the benefit of all.

www.ingramcontent.com/pod-product-compliance
Lightning Source LLC
Chambersburg PA
CBHW080551060326
40689CB00021B/4818